MW00812859

preschool
beyond walls

Blending Early Childhood Education and Nature-Based Learning

Rachel A. Larimore

Gryphon House
Lewisville, NC

Copyright

© 2019 Rachel Larimore

Published by Gryphon House, Inc.

P. O. Box 10, Lewisville, NC 27023

800.638.0928; 877.638.7576 [fax]

Visit us on the web at www.gryphonhouse.com.

All rights reserved. No part of this publication may be reproduced or transmitted in any form or by any means, electronic or technical, including photocopy, recording, or any information storage or retrieval system, without prior written permission of the publisher. Printed in the United States. Every effort has been made to locate copyright and permission information.

Cover images used under license from Shutterstock.com and courtesy of the author.

Library of Congress Cataloging-in-Publication Data

The cataloging-in-publication data is registered with the Library of Congress for ISBN 978-0-87659-794-1.

Bulk Purchase

Gryphon House books are available for special premiums and sales promotions as well as for fundraising use. Special editions or book excerpts also can be created to specifications. For details, call 800.638.0928.

Disclaimer

Gryphon House, Inc., cannot be held responsible for damage, mishap, or injury incurred during the use of or because of activities in this book. Appropriate and reasonable caution and adult supervision of children involved in activities and corresponding to the age and capability of each child involved are recommended at all times. Do not leave children unattended at any time. Observe safety and caution at all times.

DEDICATION

To all the "pocketknife kids" in my life,
and to Stuart—the tradition lives on.

CONTENTS

FOREWORD

By Claire Warden

This comprehensive book, written by an experienced, deeply reflective colleague, will support you in increasing the profile of the natural world in your early childhood setting. It creates a thought-provoking journey not only for people who are new to the field, but also for those who have been in this field for some time.

We know that children flourish in the natural world. There is more than enough research to justify nature-based encounters for play and learning within our buildings, in outdoor play areas, and in wilder spaces beyond them. When we work in rhythm with nature and the weather, we open up so many opportunities for children to learn. As the nature-based early childhood education movement grows, we create a professional network through reflective practice and wider reading. This book is based on extensive experience and research in an American context, but it also has a wider relevance to people in this field all over the world.

Part I starts by creating a clear foundation to raise awareness and understanding of nature-based preschools. These chapters examine the philosophical and pedagogical values that drive and guide the practice in these settings and the impact those values have on operational aspects. This section of the book also acknowledges that the natural world increases the complexity of our spaces, and various sections discuss risk management and hazard minimization.

The whole of part II explores the three classroom areas of inside, outside, and beyond. Each space has a unique way of shaping the relationship between the child and the environment. Rachel guides the reader clearly through the steps required to create nature-based spaces that explore opportunities for all the developmental domains.

Collaboration—between teachers and children, between members of teaching teams, and between teachers and families—supports the connection between children's experiences at school and their leisure time. It is fitting that Rachel places this section last, as she practices her belief that we need to set both children and families up for success in nature-based preschools.

Rachel's voice comes clearly through this wonderful book, which gave me a sense of being with her on the journey to increase the time our youngest children spend in the natural world. I thoroughly recommend this book to you and hope you enjoy reading it as much as I have.

C Warden

CLAIRE WARDEN

ACKNOWLEDGMENTS

I believe we learn and create by interacting with others. This book is no exception. The content is the result of years of interactions with other educators, and the book itself is the result of assistance from a talented group of editors, colleagues, friends, and family. I'm incredibly grateful for the support of each and every one of these people.

First and foremost, thank you to Gryphon House for stepping beyond the traditional bounds of early childhood education and agreeing to publish this manuscript. I am particularly grateful for the editorial support of Stephanie Roselli and Candice Bellows. They knew just how to smooth out the rough edges without losing the spirit of the words—or bringing me to tears.

Second, I owe a huge thank-you to those in the nature-based early childhood education community who have taught me a great deal about this approach to teaching young children. I continue to learn from these amazing educators who, through their own great work, challenge and help refine my thinking. Thank you to the Chippewa Nature Center, the Dodge Nature Center, Ferntop Preschool, Fiddleheads Forest School, and the Schlitz Nature Center for sharing photos and stories for this book.

This is not only an amazing community of colleagues, but many of them have become close friends as well. There are a few colleagues for whom I am particularly grateful in the writing of this book. The many teachers and staff of the Chippewa Nature Center's Nature Preschool have been instrumental in my journey in nature-based early childhood education. They have inspired, challenged, and supported me every step of the way. My good friend Claire Warden not only wrote the foreword but also received late-night texts requesting feedback or thoughts (hey, there's a time difference between the States and Scotland!). I'm grateful for the many conversations we've shared about nature-based approaches, yet I'm most grateful for all the laughter we've shared over the years. Thanks to Dave Catlin for being the kind of business partner and friend who knows just when to ask the tough questions to help me refine my thinking. I am also incredibly grateful for the leadership, mentorship, and friendship of nature-based education guru Dr. Patti Bailie.

We all need people in our lives to remind us to lighten up, have fun, and not take ourselves too seriously. I'm incredibly fortunate to have a crazy crew of people like this. Additional thanks to Danielle, Dennis, Shelley, Jessica, Herb, Gary, Deb M., Tracey, Mike, and Emily for always responding to stress-filled phone calls and texts; knowing when to keep me humble by reminding me of ridiculous things I've done over the years (there are only one or two things, tops!); knowing when to be my cheerleaders; and knowing when I need live music and a stiff drink. Thanks, Hank, for the unconditional love and humor you constantly provide.

Finally, thanks to my family—those gone too soon and those still here—who instilled in me a love for the outdoors from the very beginning. Leading the charge were my mom and dad. I'm so grateful to them for my mud-filled childhood. I'm also grateful they allowed me to park myself on the porch of their cabin for book writing—no better backdrop for writing about children and nature.

INTRODUCTION

Children need experiences in nature for their physical, cognitive, social-emotional, and spiritual health. Reciprocally, the natural world needs children to protect and care for it. These seem like lofty statements, but there is mounting evidence that both are undeniably true.

Why Children Need Nature

In recent years these ideas have been gaining momentum and increased conversation. In 2005, Richard Louv published his book *Last Child in the Woods: Saving Our Children from Nature-Deficit Disorder*, documenting the various studies from the fields of psychology, kinesiology (the study of the mechanics of body movement), education, and so forth. While his book was not a new idea for nature-based education professionals, it brought the discussion of children and nature to the mainstream. Suddenly people were talking about children's increased time in front of screens, the lack of free play in their lives, and the power of time spent in nature to support their development. In 2012, Regina Milteer and her colleagues at the American Academy of Pediatrics (AAP) affirmed that play is vital to children's development.

Additionally, researchers have been learning lessons about the benefits of outdoor play specifically. Regarding physical development, Pooja Tandon, Brian Saelens, and Dimitri Christakis found that children are more active in outdoor settings. Ingunn Fjørtoft discovered that natural play areas better support children's balance and coordination. In separate studies, Kathryn Rose and Pei-Chang Wu and their colleagues learned that time spent outdoors protects children against myopia (nearsightedness). Evidence has also been mounting regarding the benefits of outdoor play for children's cognitive development. According to researchers Cynthia Klemmer, Tina Waliczek, and Jayne Zajicek, children develop scientific knowledge through time spent learning outdoors. Andrea Faber Taylor and Frances Kuo found that outdoor play improves children's ability to concentrate. Part of concentration is self-regulatory skills, a component of children's social-emotional development, which nature has also been shown to support, as demonstrated by Faber Taylor, Kuo, and William Sullivan. Being located "nearby" nature, according to Nancy Wells and Gary Evans, can mitigate children's overall life stress. Deborah Schein learned that nature also provides moments of wonder, joy, and inner peace, which support a child's spiritual development. In two studies, Louise Chawla concluded that the social-emotional and spiritual connections that come with frequent, positive experiences with nature are part of developing children's pro-environmental behaviors. While these study results are informative, Julie Davis and Sue Elliott point out that we do need more research regarding the interplay of time spent outdoors as a young child and environmental sustainability behaviors later in life.

This is just a sampling of the growing body of evidence of the need for nature in children's lives, far from a thorough or exhaustive review. If you're interested in learning more, I encourage you to visit the Children and Nature Network's website at www.childrenandnature.org, where they have a comprehensive research database to browse. In the meantime, it is fair to say, based on a review of research literature by researcher Tim Gill, that there is clear evidence pointing to the need for nature early in children's lives.

The Movement to Reconnect

The great news is there are many parents and educators throughout the world vowing to do better for young children—to reverse the trend of children's disconnect from nature. This may be a reaction to the growing presence of technology in our world, a greater awareness of the physical and psychological implications of a disconnect from nature, or simply a desire by parents to provide children with a childhood more like their own. Whatever the reason, there is a growing interest to ensure children have regular experiences with the natural world separate from the chaotic, indoor-focused adult world. As a result, parents and educators are implementing nature-based interventions. In most cases, this is happening on a smaller and more individual level. There are, however, ways to make more large-scale changes in children's connection to the outdoors. These primarily involve community-wide efforts such as city planning and, as you might imagine, education systems. One such effort is the integration of nature into early childhood education, particularly through the implementation of nature-based preschools (NBPs). These schools have the dual goals of educating children in developmentally appropriate ways and fostering environmentally sustainable behavior.

NBPs are a relatively new but quickly growing concept in the United States. While the first American program was established in 1967 at New Canaan Nature Center in Connecticut, there were only twelve other programs in operation by 2010. Today that number has grown to more than 250, according to the North American Association for Environmental Education. Meanwhile, professional associations such as the Natural Start Alliance (www.naturalstart.org), the Northern Illinois Nature Preschool Association (www. ninpa.org), and the International Association of Nature Pedagogy (www.naturepedagogy.com) have formed to support nature-based educators. Additionally, higher education institutions are beginning to integrate nature-based approaches into their course offerings. Antioch University, for example, has established a graduate certificate in nature-based early childhood education.

At the same time as this rapid growth in NBPs, the integration of nature into the traditional preschool classroom has also become a popular topic. It seems it's impossible to attend an early childhood education conference these days without seeing at least one session on the agenda related to nature. There is, however, a wide range in how these workshops define and advocate for the presence, value, and integration of nature in the classroom. I've seen conference sessions focused on making art with natural materials, exhibit halls selling plastic playground equipment made to look like natural logs, and activity books emphasizing the didactic instruction of nature facts. That being said, I've also seen some really wonderful examples of teachers who are authentically connecting young children to nature. For this reason, I always caution early childhood professionals to be good consumers of any professional development focused on nature integration (or of professional development on any topic, for that matter).

Making the Dream a Reality

Part of making the dream of an NBP a reality is getting support and buy-in along the way. If you're starting an NBP from the ground up, it's relatively easy to get buy-in because you will hire staff and attract families who share the vision. Harder, though, is making a shift in an existing program toward a nature-based approach. Making change starts with interactions with the individual child, then class- and team-level changes, and finally the program as a whole. The control you have over changes to the program will depend on the responsibilities you carry and your circle of influence. If you are a teacher, create goals for yourself and your teaching team. If you are a middle manager, work with the teachers within your influence. If you are the program director or administrator for the entire organization, then look at making organization-wide changes. No matter your role, you have the ability to make small, significant changes in practice that will move you toward the nature-based approach we'll discuss throughout this book.

Making these small shifts will be easier and have a greater impact if you have buy-in from coworkers. It's important to acknowledge up front, however, that getting complete buy-in may take time. Start with the "low-hanging fruit"—the simplest changes to make—and build from there. One approach I've seen succeed is to start with one team that is interested in being more nature-based. Administrators then allocate additional funds for equipment and supplies to get the interested team started, provide some specialized professional development related to the nature-based approach, and then support them in making changes throughout the year. This one team's success will inspire others and also provide insights into organizational needs to implement the approach in other classrooms. If you're an administrator struggling to find a team that's willing, consider providing a financial (or other) incentive to implement the new approach.

Hopefully, as you read this book, the possible small changes in practice will become more evident. Perhaps you will start by adding more natural elements indoors, shift to starting your day outside in the natural play area, or hire someone to provide a workshop for your staff about the nature-based approach. It does not matter where you begin—just that you begin. So identify your underlying philosophy, your desired vision, and gaps between your current practice and your vision; establish measurable goals to achieving the vision; and then get to work in changing your practice. This is the essence of being an intentional teacher and administrator.

How This Book Can Help

Through my years of providing many nature-based professional-development workshops for early childhood educators, I have heard all sorts of questions and concerns. Here are just a few:

- "What do you do in the rain?"
- "So do you worry about the kids running off?"
- "My boss told me I needed to use the TV more because we received a grant to fund it."
- "I was told we couldn't have picnic tables in our outdoor play area."

While the specific questions and concerns at these workshops may vary, they seem to be grouped into two main categories. The two questions are examples of what I hear from skeptical teachers or administrators. I believe these educators really do understand that children need time in the outdoors, but they're struggling to see how the nature component fits into their current approach to early childhood education. The two concerns, on the other hand, are the type I hear from teachers who are desperate to move away from the traditional approach to early childhood education and toward a more nature-based approach. Unfortunately, many of these teachers find themselves battling administrators, coworkers, or—worst of all— unwritten policies that seem to pervade organizational cultures.

One of the reasons this book is important is to help educators like you determine what an authentic nature-based experience is and how you can make that happen in your program. Part of this process is reflecting on where you and your program already are in the process of nature integration, so you know where you have opportunities for growth. It's also important to know what real and perceived barriers exist in implementing this pedagogy, or way of teaching children. The goal of this book is to help you identify those opportunities and potential barriers, while also describing possible action steps.

There are chapters in this book focused on the teacher and families, but there is no chapter focused on the child. The reason for this is quite simple: Children are primed and ready for learning outdoors. All they need is a safe, supportive environment in which to play and explore. From the child's perspective, it's really quite simple—let's go outside and play! Adults, on the other hand, have had a lifetime to worry, analyze, and create worst-case scenarios in their heads. In other words, if programs are going to be more nature-based, the energy is most likely going to be focused on changing the adults' attitudes and behaviors.

This book focuses on just that: helping early childhood professionals, administrators and teachers alike, to change practices to more fully integrate nature into their programs. I recognize that not every preschool in the United States (or the world, for that matter) will become an NBP. However, I believe that any program can increase its integration of nature and reap the benefits.

My last book, *Establishing a Nature-Based Preschool*, was designed to help organizations and individuals who were looking to start an NBP from scratch and most likely were operating within the environmental education discipline, such as nature centers. Since that book was published, I've had many preschool teachers and administrators ask for ideas for integrating nature into their existing preschool programs. These professionals understand early childhood education, but they want to better understand how to make nature a part of their practice. My goal in writing this book is to provide these teachers and administrators with real, tangible ideas for integrating nature into preschool programs that are already in operation.

To accomplish this goal, this book starts broad and then narrows as we go. We start by discussing the overall theory and philosophy behind NBPs. Then we move into discussing the pedagogy in more detail, including structuring the physical environment. Finally, we pull everything together in terms of daily planning and working with families. Each chapter includes background information, tangible examples of those concepts in action, answers to frequently asked questions, and "Reflections on Practice" prompts to encourage you to think about your current practice and opportunities to move toward a nature-based approach. Again, my hope is that this book will provide steps for educators to integrate nature into their teaching to enhance the high-quality early childhood practices they are already implementing. After all, children deserve authentic, meaningful experiences with the natural world on an ongoing basis.

PART I:
LAYING THE FOUNDATION

This first section of the book lays the foundation for the nature-based approach. First, we discuss exactly what is meant by *nature-based preschool,* so we know what we are moving toward. Second, to be effective in implementing anything new in the classroom, it's vital to understand the "why" behind those changes. We discuss the underpinning philosophy and pedagogy of the nature-based approach. We then conclude this section with a discussion of the practical concerns of implementing this approach while adhering to licensing regulations and ensuring children's safety.

Chapter 1:
WHAT IS A NATURE-BASED PRESCHOOL?

Nature-based preschools (NBPs) are part of a broader category known as nature-based early childhood education (NbECE), which refers to any program that combines practices from early childhood education and environmental education. There are a variety of programs within NbECE, but this book focuses solely on NBPs, which fully integrate the best practices of each discipline into a unique pedagogy. The result is an approach much greater than the sum of its parts.

Given the benefits children reap from nature, in my ideal world every preschool would be a full-fledged NBP. While I may be more optimistic about changing the world than some, I am not completely naïve. I realize this is not a realistic goal. I do believe a realistic goal is moving all programs *toward* full integration.

Almost any program providing early childhood programming is somewhere on a continuum of integrating nature. You may, for example, bring interesting plants and animals into your classroom for the children to examine. You probably provide books about nature, including informational texts on everything from trees to grass to water to birds to unique ecosystems like tallgrass prairies or coral reefs. You may take the children on field trips to local parks or to a zoo. If so, that's great! This book is primarily focused on helping you move your program even further along the continuum toward becoming an NBP than you already are. However, before moving into suggestions for changing current practices, it's important to first understand early childhood education and environmental education as separate disciplines and then to see how those disciplines are integrated.

Where Early Childhood Education and Environmental Education Meet

The first eight years of a child's life is a period of incredible cognitive, physical, social-emotional, and spiritual development. Teaching in early childhood is guided by developmentally appropriate practice, as outlined by Carol Copple and Sue Bredekamp, which emphasizes learning through play. Many programs utilize an emergent-curriculum approach, in which teachers plan activities and projects based on the interests, needs, and skills of the specific group of children they are working with. Supporting the love of learning, curiosity, and sense of wonder early on is critical for children's happiness and lifelong success. There is mounting evidence that play-based, child-centered approaches to early childhood education support later academic success. The good news is that the NBP approach is rooted in a play-based, emergent curriculum that emphasizes discovery and wonder!

Environmental education (EE), broadly speaking, is focused on developing individuals who are stewards of the planet. To accomplish this goal, EE includes knowledge, skills, and emotional connections to lead to pro-environmental behaviors. EE in the early years focuses primarily on discovery and wonder about the natural world; builds individuals' comfort outdoors; and lays the foundation for a lifelong connection with the natural world—helping children develop pro-environmental behaviors.

Where the disciplines of early childhood and environmental education meet is NbECE. This type of experience is much more than an early childhood program that happens to meet outside. Learning is not just occurring *in* nature, but nature is infused into all aspects of learning and central to the pedagogy. NbECE programs include full-time, outdoor programs such as forest kindergartens and waldkindergartens, as well as NBPs. This book is focused on developing NBPs. While there are many possibilities for the structure and operation of an NBP, my goal is to outline what I believe is the ideal NBP so that, wherever your starting point is, you can move toward that approach.

So what makes an NBP different from a traditional preschool? Historically, NBPs were primarily housed at nature centers, but the variety of business structures is constantly growing. There are farm-based programs, programs at universities, programs at zoos, public-private partnerships, and much more. In the end, what is most important is not the administrative or financial structure but the pedagogy within the program.

NBPs fully integrate the best practices of early childhood education with the best practices of EE. They are a type of licensed program for three- to five-year-olds, with at least 30 percent of each class day (whether it is part- or full-day) held outside. Nature is the driving theme and is infused into all parts of the experience. Claire Warden, author of *Learning with Nature*, refers to the spaces at an NBP as the indoors, the outdoors, and what she calls "the beyond": the natural areas away from the school. NBPs emphasize building relationships with the natural world through extensive daily outdoor experiences and whole-child development through a child-centered, emergent curriculum that focuses on nature.

Pedagogy of Nature-Based Preschools: An Overview

Being operated by a nature center does not make a preschool nature based. Having a preschool near a natural area does not necessarily make it nature based either. Having an outdoor play area with some natural materials also does not make a program nature based. So what does? The key to a nature-based approach is the day-to-day program practices—both structure and process—which come together to create the nature-based pedagogy. This means any program, if intentional about teaching and administrative practices, can be nature based. In other words, *your* program can be nature based as well!

Goals

NBPs have two primary goals: educating children in developmentally appropriate ways and teaching environmental stewardship. This means we want to support young children's development in all domains: physical, social-emotional, and cognitive. This includes the subdomains within these areas, such as spiritual and aesthetic development. At the same time, NBPs strive to develop children's meaningful connection with the natural world, laying the foundation for the development of environmentally sustainable behaviors. For a nature-based approach, the connection to the natural world is not just one of many child development goals, but one of the most significant. After all, it's this blending of the two disciplines—early childhood and environmental education—that creates NbECE.

Learning Spaces

Regular access to the physical environment is the first critical component to the NBP approach, and the structure of that physical space is the second. In an NBP, learning occurs indoors, outdoors in a natural play area, and in wilder spaces beyond the play area—inside, outside, and beyond. To illustrate, imagine for a moment this preschool.

As they arrive at school, the parents and children each sign in for the day in ways appropriate for their ages, deposit backpacks in the children's cubbies indoors, and then head outside to join the teachers. They slowly meander along a curvy, wooded path, fallen leaves crunching underfoot, as they make their way to the outdoor play area. There they are greeted by smiling teachers dressed in hats, mittens, and core layers. Children spot their friends at favorite spots like the sandbox, mud kitchen, digging hill, or other natural elements. With a quick "Bye!" to her parents, the newest arrival runs off to join her friends, rain suit swishing as she moves. Loose parts, such as sticks, buckets, and PVC pipes, become ramps, forts, traps to capture bad guys, and more. Teachers join in the fun, either playing alongside the children or joining as partners in play.

After about an hour, a teacher moves around the play area informing the children that play will wrap up in five more minutes. Children scurry to fill as much fun as they can into those minutes before the teacher shakes the squirrel call, signaling everyone to meet at the stump circle. Each person claims a stump as part of the group circle.

One teacher officially welcomes each student, acknowledging guests who have joined the class for the day and wishing well those students who are absent. After the welcome, the teacher leans into the circle and excitedly whispers, "Guess where we're going on our hike today?" Children's voices, full of hopeful conviction, shout out their favorite places—the meadow! the sand hill! the pond! "Those are all wonderful places that we'll visit again soon, but today we're going to the forest."

After discussing tools to take along for forest exploration, safety gear to carry on the trail, and counting the number of people, the group heads off. One teacher leads the pack, which loosely resembles a line. Another brings up the rear, and the third teacher and other adults help in the middle—all conversing with the children as they happily walk, skip, or jump along the trail. At the destination, safety is once again discussed, boundaries are designated, and tools are made accessible. Exploration of the forest begins. Mirrors, spoons, bug boxes, and other tools are in full use as the children peek under mushrooms, lift logs, and touch tree bark.

Once the children have had sufficient time to explore, the teachers once again use the squirrel call to gather the group, reflect on their findings, and slowly make their way back to the preschool building. As the group enters the building, the feel of the outdoors follows them.

The rooms have a natural appearance with wood furniture, soft neutral colors on the walls, and the morning sun pouring through the large windows. Some children pull off their rain suits in one quick motion, showing this is not their first transition from outdoors to indoors. Other children slowly remove one item at a time, telling stories of their adventures to their neighbors. As they finish changing, the children zip into the classroom to find a spot at a table to begin a family-style snack, where they'll share even more tales of their morning adventure. With full tummies, they will finish their day with choice time and a small group activity inside the classroom.

The low window sill invites children to observe squirrels feasting at the bird feeders or to gaze out at the trees beyond. The materials throughout the classroom include a variety of nature-related items such as seed and rock collections, child-sized dress-up butterfly wings, birding vests, and binoculars. The puzzles have images of local wildlife and plants. The library includes storybooks about discovering nature and field guides to learn more about the local birds, wildflowers, and animal tracks. Pinecones, pine needles, acorns, dried corn, and a basket of leaves are situated among the paints, cotton balls, and yarn in the art area.

After playing in the classroom, the group gathers for one final story followed by the goodbye song. Teachers dismiss the children to find their parents and make their way along the same wooded path that had greeted them three hours before.

In this scenario, play occurs in three distinct spaces that reflect the local natural world. Each of these three spaces—inside, outside, and beyond—plays an important role. Ideally, the line between the outdoors and indoors is blurred. Through materials and teacher-child interactions, learning is connected to the experiences children have in the outdoors and beyond. The natural play area outdoors provides a variety of human-made and natural loose parts to create a rich learning space in support of all developmental domains. The beyond space then provides a wilder experience that is less predictable than the indoor and outdoor spaces—what will nature present to us today? The three distinct spaces (inside, outside, and beyond) vary in their amounts of human structure and dominance, with the inside being the most human-structured and the beyond the least.

According to Patti Bailie in the book *Nature Play and Learning Places*, children in NBPs are outside every day for *at least* 30 percent of the class session. A three-hour session would be outside for at least one hour; a six-hour program would be outside at least two hours. Many nature-based programs are outside much longer; in fact, many stay outside the entire day for several days out of the school year. The only exception to extensive, daily outdoor time is if the weather is dangerous. *Dangerous* means lightning, severe cold, extremely high winds, and so on. *Dangerous* does not mean rainy days or days when the temperatures drop below zero. After all, appropriate clothing can make rainy weather and cold temperatures quite pleasant for play.

Of course, this daily outdoor time is not simply to see how tough children are and whether they can tolerate being outdoors in all conditions. Rather, the purpose of daily outdoor time is to provide positive and meaningful play opportunities for children. There is joy in jumping in a mud puddle. There is wonder in catching falling snowflakes on a mitten and deciding whether each snowflake really is unique. Daily outdoor time is an opportunity to see the wonder of the world in all its various states and to marvel at the different details that emerge in the sun, rain, snow, heat, and cold.

Emergent Curriculum

In addition to the three dimensions of the physical environment, a core component of NBP pedagogy is an emergent curriculum. An emergent curriculum is founded on daily, responsive planning and teacher-child interactions that extend and build on children's interests. With so much outdoor time, the curriculum becomes rooted in what is happening seasonally as the natural world sparks children's interests.

The seasonal, authentic experiences, along with the children's interests, lead to studies that move inside, outside, beyond, and back again. One group of children, for example, might have discovered hundreds of worms crawling in and out of the spring soil. That is a seasonal happening that has piqued the children's interest. In the outdoor play area, teachers could provide additional buckets and spoons for collecting the worms. On an excursion beyond the play area, teachers might take along a dry-erase board for counting worms they find on the hike. Inside, a small group activity could be to create a worm racetrack, leading to conversations, predictions, and observations about which worm will make it to the finish line first and why. Of course, part of learning about worms is learning to treat them gently and return them to their habitat when the exploration is finished. The teachers allow the children's interests to guide the activities, and the teachers extend that learning to integrate multiple objectives.

Part of what defines an NBP is the intentional blending of experiences in nature with teaching practices. I'm sure as an early childhood educator you've heard people ask something along the lines of, "Oh, so all the children do all day is just play?" For most early childhood educators, this is about as nerve-racking as fingernails on a chalkboard, because we know that play is learning. I have a similar reaction to comments such as, "Oh, so you *just* go for a walk in the woods." Ack! Technically, yes, they're playing or walking in the woods, but high-quality educators help scaffold children's learning through observations, questions, and reflections. A walk in the woods may not have a predetermined destination, but the objective is always predetermined—children's learning.

Teachers

An amazing physical environment and wonderful lesson plans are only part of supporting children's learning. The elements that will make or break a program in terms of quality learning are the interactions that happen among teachers and children. The role of NBP teachers is to connect the children's experiences throughout the days and weeks and in each of the three physical areas. Conversations and questions in an NBP encourage and support children's learning, and they balance providing information with allowing children to discover answers for themselves. At their core, these interactions demonstrate the value placed on children. They are seen as capable, competent, and full of opinions and interests. Teachers in NBPs value children's thoughts and ideas, a practice that inherently makes these programs child centered.

Teaching in an NBP means providing opportunities for learning *in*, *about*, and *with* nature, with the primary emphasis on learning *with* nature.

Licensing

You'll notice that NBPs are defined as being licensed programs. Some in NbECE have questioned the need for licensing as part of defining an NBP. I recognize that in some states programs are able to operate without being licensed. Some states do not license programs because there is no physical facility or the program operates below a certain threshold of contact hours. For example, as I mentioned earlier, forest preschools often operate without a license. I give programs the benefit of the doubt and assume not that they are trying to skirt the rules but that their states lack rules to which they may adhere. After all, most licensing regulations focus heavily on indoor facilities, so programs like forest preschools leave licensing inspectors unsure how to proceed.

In a step toward addressing this problem, the state of Washington recently passed legislation to create licensing regulations for all-outdoor preschools. I'm hopeful Washington's efforts will encourage other states to develop licensing regulations for preschool programs operating with limited physical space. After all, it's still vital that NbECE programs operate in a way that is safe and responsive to children's needs. Licensing regulations establish minimum standards of safety and quality and provide a system to verify adherence to those standards.

My hope is that you now have a clear vision of what a quality NBP looks like in action. This will guide the next several chapters as I provide suggestions for making the shift from traditional approaches to early childhood education to a nature-based approach. For some traditional preschools, shifting practice to a truly emergent, child-centered curriculum with three distinct learning environments may take extensive work, but it is possible to make changes in practices!

Frequently Asked Questions

1. **Why should I establish an NBP instead of a traditional preschool? What can this type of program teach children that they cannot learn elsewhere?** NBPs achieve the same learning outcomes as traditional preschools by helping children build authentic, meaningful connections to the natural world around them. In this way, children's whole development is addressed. Significantly, NBPs also provide deep social-emotional and spiritual development as children experience the wonders of the world and something greater than themselves.

2. **How much does it cost to convert a preschool to an NBP?** The financial costs of converting an existing preschool to a nature-based approach are minimal. There will likely be some expenses for equipment and materials and for professional development for staff. Most of the challenge, however, of converting a preschool will be in adjusting the community culture within your program: the attitudes and behaviors of administrators, teachers, parents, and children. If you rush the process of culture change, relationships can be damaged, so go slowly, be patient, and be transparent in the process.

3. **How long will it take to start an NBP from scratch versus converting an existing program into an NBP?** As mentioned earlier, the biggest challenge in converting an existing program is changing community culture, which takes a lot of time. You can start right now with small changes. The more of them you make, the more quickly you'll move along the continuum of nature-based practice. Remember, however, that this is not a race. The point is to create positive, effective learning environments for young children. This result comes from making intentional decisions in administration and teaching on a daily basis. Take your time, and in a year or two you'll look back and be amazed at just how far you've come.

4. **How can an emergent curriculum possibly cover all the content and skills listed in my state's regulations for this age group?** Emergent curriculum is hard work—no question. It is possible, however, to cover the content and skills in early learning standards through emergent curriculum. Daily planning is responsive not only to children's interests but also to curricular goals. In other words, as you plan, you consider not only what subjects and activities the children are interested in but also how you can embed the required content and skills within those subjects and activities.

Reflections on Practice

1. What is the role of nature in my program's philosophy?

2. What value does my program place on nature? How is that exhibited through policy and day-to-day procedures?

3. What do I want the value and role of nature to be in my program philosophy?

4. What questions do I have about starting an NBP, whether doing it from scratch or by converting an existing program?

5. What is my tolerance level for weather, insects, animals, dirt, and other common natural features? What are the tolerance levels of the other staff members in my program?

Chapter 2:
ESTABLISHING YOUR PROGRAM'S PHILOSOPHY AND PEDAGOGY

Yogi Berra once said, "If you don't know where you're going, you'll end up someplace else." That idea applies to making changes in early childhood practices. Having a clear vision of where you're headed is critical for successful change. Otherwise, you'll end up someplace other than an NBP.

Defining Terms

Any NBP (or any school, for that matter) needs a mission statement, a program philosophy, a set of policies, and its own pedagogy. Each component is a critical part of how your NBP is defined and functions.

- A *mission statement* describes the primary purpose of your program. This statement is generally written in a form like this: "The mission of the Children's Preschool is to provide a safe, educational learning environment for young children." An NBP's mission statement might read like this: "The mission of Sprouts Nature Preschool is to provide a premier early childhood environment that meets the developmental needs of the whole child while initiating children into a lifelong, meaningful relationship with the natural world." Everything that happens in your program should be in pursuit of the goal outlined in your mission statement.

- A *program philosophy* is a detailed description of why and how you bring your mission statement to life. It is the set of values that underpins policies and daily procedures—the rationale for *why* and *how* certain things are done in your organization. The thousands of daily decisions that teachers and administrators make are rooted in their program's philosophy. The challenge is sorting out the reasons behind those decisions and making sure that that reasoning is consistent across all policies and situations. To make that consistency possible, you need to create a written philosophy statement in addition to your mission statement.

- *Policies* explain what to do in particular situations. Policies are typically compiled in manuals that instruct teachers and administrators on how to handle everything from the daily schedule to sudden emergencies. We'll talk more about these useful documents later in this book.

- *Pedagogy* refers to how the teaching is done in your program. All NBPs have certain aspects of pedagogy in common, which we discuss later in this book.

Together, all of these components determine how an NBP functions from day to day and why it functions that way. For example, let's return to the sample NBP mission statement from earlier: "The mission of Sprouts Nature Preschool is to provide a premier early childhood environment that meets the developmental needs of the whole child while initiating children into a lifelong, meaningful relationship with the natural world." To support this goal, a policy at this school might say that all snacks will be provided by the school. The underpinning philosophy for this policy might be any of these ideas:

- Balanced nutrition is essential, and thus our program will ensure that healthy snacks are provided to the children.

- We seek to create an equitable space in our preschool, where no child has less or more than another child.

- Because we want to maximize the time spent in play and learning, it is more efficient to provide snacks to the children than to spend time retrieving brought-from-home food from backpacks or cubbies at snack time.

Finally, the act of providing the snacks is also part of this NBP's pedagogy because it teaches the children the values contained in the underpinning philosophy.

Whether you are converting an existing program to an NBP or starting an NBP from scratch, you will need to make sure your mission statement, program philosophy, policies, and pedagogy are compatible with the values and practices of NbECE. Let's examine some of these components more closely.

Establishing Your Philosophy

Even if you're a teacher and are not directly responsible for establishing a program philosophy, this section is still relevant. As educators, we should all have a clear understanding of our own beliefs about how young children should be taught. This will ensure that we are working in a way that is true to ourselves.

In the previous chapter, I describe NbECE as the integration of early childhood and environmental education. Those two broad categories are a good starting point for establishing your philosophy of nature-based education. First, there are questions to ask yourself about early childhood education in any setting. Second, there are questions to ask yourself about early childhood education in a nature-based setting. But before getting into the specifics of these questions, let's talk a bit about the process of establishing a program philosophy.

Involving Your Staff in the Process

If you're an administrator, your approach to establishing your program's philosophy will be rooted in your personal administrative style. There are thousands of books on administrative style, but they generally agree that the more involvement staff have in the process of establishing an organization's philosophy, the greater their buy-in. Thus, you'll want to engage your staff in the process of evaluating and establishing your program's philosophy as you answer the questions in the rest of this chapter. Suddenly springing an entirely new philosophy on your staff will probably be met with resistance. A onetime retreat can provide an opportunity to craft a philosophy together, but a better approach would be to discuss the questions in this chapter casually for some time, perhaps even over a year or two, and then have one or more whole-staff consensus-building activities to definitively answer the questions for your program. Again, the specifics will depend on your administrative style, but the point is that staff investment in the process will lead to success.

Once you have consensus on your philosophy statement, write it down and distribute copies to the entire staff so that everyone is on the same page (literally and figuratively) about why you do what you do in your program.

Standard Components of NBP Philosophy

While each NBP will have unique aspects to its philosophy, some components will be present in the philosophy of any NBP. NBPs are rooted in the belief that outdoor experiences are critical to whole-child development. These outdoor experiences provide children with the opportunity to learn from the natural world, seeing nature as a teacher. The outdoor experiences also build a sense of place. Thus, NBPs prioritize connection to local place rather than to distant places. In practice, for example, this means focusing on local plants and animals rather than those from far-off lands. Developing a sense of place also means connecting to the culture, or human elements, of the local community. Connection to the local place leads to a sense of responsibility for that place and a desire to preserve the local environment. This idea of environmental sustainability is another core value of NBPs.

Despite these common themes, there is a wide variety of philosophies within NBPs, just as there is within early childhood education in general. Given these nuances, it's important that all staff and families understand the philosophical basis for the decisions made and the practices enacted in your program. Whether you are an administrator or a teacher, that basis is formed as you answer certain questions about early childhood education in general and about the nature-based approach specifically. The next several sections discuss these questions.

Questions about Early Childhood Education in General

For any early childhood program, it's important to determine *whom* you would like to serve, *how* you want to serve them, and, of course, *why* you want to serve them. The answers to each question have many practical implications for your program.

Determining whom to serve can include a variety of demographics. Will you only serve three- and four-year-olds, or would you like to serve infants and toddlers as well? How diverse would you like the school population to be? What does *diversity* mean to you? Does diversity include variations in economics, ethnicity, and geography? Does it include children with special needs? With each of these questions, there is also a vital follow-up question—why? Why is serving these different populations important to you? Answering the "why" will inform a plethora of administrative decisions, such as whether to offer scholarships or employ therapists on staff.

Once you've determined whom you will serve, the next step is to determine how you will serve them. What is the role of the teacher in your program? In this book, I describe the teacher as a co-learner alongside the children, but maybe that does not fit entirely with your view of adult-child interactions. Part of these adult-child interactions is being clear in what you believe young children should be allowed or encouraged to do. What do you believe young children are capable of and not capable of? Are there things you believe children should not be allowed to do? Another adult-child interaction to think about is the role of parents. What role do you believe parents should play in children's education and in your preschool in particular?

Questions about Nature-Based Early Childhood Education

The questions in the previous section are important in any setting, and there are also philosophical questions to answer related to nature-based settings in particular. The most significant, and perhaps obvious, question is why. Why do you believe children need experiences with nature? But that is only the first of many questions. What should these experiences entail? How frequently should they occur? With whom should they take place?

I encourage you to dig deeply when answering these questions. As an example, here is how I would answer the question of why children need experiences with nature: At the opening of this book, I describe the power of nature to influence children's overall development. I often cite child development as a reason for doing this work, and that is true. If I dig more deeply into my own philosophy, however, the foundational reason I do this work is that I love the natural world and all of its beauty and wonder. I believe that we as humans have an obligation to care for the planet, and I believe the way we do that is by helping children build an emotional and intellectual connection with nature from an early age.

Thus, when you're answering the "Why nature?" question, really push yourself to get to your core, foundational reason for doing this work. The wonderful thing is we will all have slightly different reasons, and yet we share a common desire to connect children to nature.

Establishing Your Policies

Once you've determined your mission statement and program philosophy, it's time to determine your vision for integrating nature into your policies, or what you do in any given situation in your program. To do this, review your program's daily structure and physical environment and make an honest assessment of how well your current policies integrate nature. (We look at pedagogy, or teaching practices, in the next section.) I provide a "Reflections on Practice" section at the end of each chapter to help you with this process, but here are a few examples of questions to be thinking about right now:

Daily Structure
- Where do the children start their day (inside or outside)?
- How much time do the children currently spend outside?

Physical Environment

Inside
- How do you integrate nature into your classroom?

- Do you have animals? Do you have plants? Can the children interact with these?

- Do you have books about local nature or related to local natural features?

- What other natural elements do you bring in? How are they used or explored by the children?

Outside
- How much time do the children currently spend outside?

- Where do they spend their outside time?

- Does the outdoor play area have the general feel of a natural space?

- How many loose parts (such as sticks, shovels, acorns, PVC pipe segments, and so on) are provided outside?

Beyond
- Do you currently take field trips with the children? Where do you go? How do you get there?

- What places are available for exploration (such as parks, nature centers, farms, and so on) in your area?

Once you have determined where your program is on the continuum of integrating nature, ask yourself where you would like to be. Do your current policies and your desired policies line up? If not, where might you make improvements? What are the barriers to achieving your goals? Identify what small steps you can take today to move toward your goals.

Establishing Your Pedagogy

Once you have a thorough understanding of your beliefs and the motivations behind your NBP, you can begin defining how you will carry out your program's mission. Here are some key components to the pedagogy (how you teach what you teach) of an NBP.

Becoming an NBP: Bridging a Pedagogical Gap with a Policy Change

I once worked with a preschool that had been trying to incorporate nature into its program for years. The staff had integrated nature indoors and provided more natural elements and loose parts in the outdoor play area, but they still felt that something was lacking. They determined that to truly achieve the nature-based approach they desired, they had to overcome a major barrier: the lack of regular visits to a beyond space. While there was a park within walking distance of the school, the staff felt that it would be too time-consuming to walk both there and back in one school day.

To solve this problem, the staff implemented a new policy. Once each week, they had family members and guardians drop off their children at the park instead of at the school. After their experience in the beyond, the teachers and children would walk back to the school for the rest of the day. By identifying the vision, the barrier, and a small shift in policy that could help them break through the barrier, this staff was able to move closer to their goals for their school.

Supporting Learning in All Domains

Part of establishing your philosophy and then implementing pedagogy is being able to articulate how your particular teaching approach supports children's development. If a parent walked into your classroom and said, "What are they learning right now?" you should be able to describe the learning that is happening in that moment.

In recent years there has been more and more pressure on preschools to develop children's academic skills—particularly related to literacy. Yes, those skills are important, but so are the other developmental domains. In fact, most states now have pre-K learning standards that outline learning that should occur across all domains. Fortunately, NBPs are uniquely positioned to support not only cognitive skills but all other domains as well, and thus meet pre-K learning standards.

Here is a breakdown of how NBPs specifically support learning in cognitive, social-emotional, physical, and spiritual domains:

- **Cognitive development:** Natural spaces allow for engagement of all of a child's senses, creative thinking, and skill and knowledge development in specific subject areas.

  - **Math:** Math is easily integrated into learning outdoors. For example, when the children notice an insect, count the number of legs with them. Look for more insects, and create a chart recording how many legs each has. With the children, examine the data they've collected and talk about what they notice.

  - **Science:** Science, too, fits easily into a nature-based program. For example, if children show an interest in birds they see outside, you can help them learn more. Bring in age-appropriate informational texts on birds. Encourage children to take photos of local birds, and then work with them to identify the species. Investigate what birds eat and where they live.

  - **Language:** Language skills will develop naturally out of the conversations you and the children have as they explore and investigate. Using diverse scientific words and a variety of adjectives to describe the natural world not only builds vocabulary but also the language around science—particularly natural history.

  - **Emerging literacy:** Not only can you bring in informational texts and other books related to the children's interests, but you can also incorporate literacy into everyday conversations and other work the children do. For example, if a child is learning about local birds, you could help the child recognize letter sounds. You might say, "Bird. *Bird* starts with the letter *b*. *B* makes the /b/ sound. /B/, /b/, bird. Let's write the letter *b* together."

  - **Arts and music explorations:** The outdoors is a fabulous place to do (potentially messy) art explorations or make music with children. For all of human history, the natural world has been inspiring artists of all kinds—including the youngest artists among us.

- **Social-emotional development:** Imaginative, loose-part play provides many opportunities for interactions and problem solving with peers.

- **Physical development:** Generally speaking, preschoolers are more active in outdoor activities and in child-directed play, as pointed out by researchers

Pooja Tandon, Brian Saelens, and Dimitri Christakis. Fortunately, natural play areas and exploration in the beyond provide many child-led, outdoor activities that help develop balance, coordination, and physical strength. Author Angela Hanscom, for example, explains in her book *Balanced and Barefoot* that physical strength, particularly in development of the body's core and activities that cross the midline of the body (involve movement from one side of the body to the other), is beneficial in its own right and is important in supporting children's ability to sit and attend to cognitive tasks.

- **Spiritual development:** Spending time in the natural world, whether in active play or in quiet reflection, gives children the opportunity to experience a world separate from the chaos of the human-made world and be part of something bigger than themselves. Deborah Schein, coauthor with Mary Rivkin of *The Great Outdoors: Advocating for Natural Spaces for Young Children*, says that the moments of wonder, joy, and inner peace that nature provides are foundational to children's spiritual development. This spiritual connection and general appreciation of and love for the natural world is part of helping children develop long-term, pro-environmental and sustainable behaviors.

Being able to articulate the learning that occurs in an authentic, play-based nature setting is part of fleshing out your philosophy. Believing in and then living a nature-based approach includes understanding *how* the nature-based approach supports whole-child development.

Emergent Curriculum

You have probably noticed that this book does not provide a variety of discrete activities to do outdoors with children. This is because a truly emergent curriculum cannot be built around prescribed activities and must be child centered. Many states now have early learning standards for the knowledge and skills we should be teaching young children. While those standards serve a purpose and are useful in reflecting on our teaching practice, I am a proponent of what researcher Lilian Katz calls "standards of experience": focusing on providing children with a variety of experiences rather than with specific bits of knowledge or skills. Katz argues these experiences support intellectual goals, which include a range of aesthetic and moral sensibilities, rather than academic goals, which she says focus on "acquiring small discrete bits of disembodied information." In terms of an early childhood curriculum, she goes on to argue that an appropriate curriculum in the early years is one that encourages and motivates children to seek mastery of basic academic skills in the service of their intellectual pursuits. NBPs should primarily support children's intellectual pursuits—their interests and ideas—by providing a variety of experiences that are meaningful to them. What each child learns from these experiences will vary based on her current development, her previous experiences, and the particular context where the experience is occurring.

So yes, I could give you a list of activities to do outdoors with children (see Appendix A for some resources), but I believe it's more valuable to provide a broad view of the pedagogy that you can use to guide your day-to-day and moment-to-moment decisions. My goal is to help guide your thinking in which activities you choose and to help you articulate why you chose those activities. So how do we create experiences for young children that emerge from their interests and ideas? There are three key answers to this question for the nature-based approach:

- Daily, responsive planning

- Mixing learning *in*, *about*, and most importantly *with* nature

- In-the-moment adjustments

Becoming an NBP: From Set Lessons to Responsive Curriculum

I once worked with a program that over the course of several years shifted its curriculum to depend on daily, responsive planning. When I began working with this school, the curriculum was based on seasonal units, and all activities were planned months in advance based on typical conditions and events for the applicable time of year. Children's interests and ideas did not come into play at all—after all, the lesson plans for the entire year were often done before the class rosters were finalized.

As I worked with the teachers at this school, they began to see that there was a better way to plan. The themes in their units became more flexible, and units began to be implemented based on weather changes rather than on set dates—for example, teachers would begin the unit on snow at the first snowfall of the year instead of on December 1—but this practice still did not leave much room to incorporate children's preferences and interests into their learning. As these teachers became more comfortable with an emergent curriculum, they eventually abandoned set units altogether. Instead of setting their teaching agendas in advance, they used what they knew about the children's current interests and the upcoming weather to formulate a general idea of what they might teach each week. Then, after school each day, they would determine the specifics of the next day's lessons.

Daily, Responsive Planning

Simply put, in emergent curriculum the curriculum *emerges* from children's interests and ideas. Planning activities months or weeks in advance is not emergent curriculum. While weekly planning can be somewhat responsive to children's interests, daily planning is the most responsive way to plan. Daily lesson plans for large-group and small-group activities, new materials in the indoor and outdoor area, and experiences in the beyond should always emerge out of what has occurred during the previous days. Keep in mind that transitions between activities should also be captured in your lesson plans and as much as possible be based on children's current interests. These activities and materials might build on something children were doing yesterday, or it might be a new direction based on something you observed children doing or an idea they expressed. By doing this responsive planning, you are centering children in the curriculum. If you are truly implementing emergent curriculum, it will naturally be child centered—a core tenet of the nature-based approach.

Ideally, daily lesson planning is done as a teaching team. This means every teacher who interacts with the children should reflect on children's learning and ways to scaffold or extend that learning. By doing so, the teaching team can capitalize on what psychologist Lev Vygotsky called the *zone of proximal development*, that space that exists between what a child can do without any help and what a child cannot do at all. Rich learning happens when we build on children's current development and challenge them just enough to support their continued growth. In a perfect world, children themselves would also have an opportunity to give input for the next class. A simple question such as, "What should we do on our hike tomorrow?" can tell you a great deal about children's interests.

Now, some of you may be saying, "But we don't have time to plan every day!" I realize for many programs planning time is limited to part of one afternoon per week, and in some cases there is no scheduled time for planning. For those programs looking to move toward a daily planning approach, I suggest generating a temporary plan for the coming week and then modifying those plans each day. This allows for flexibility based on the children and the weather while keeping the daily planning time to a minimum. But again, ideally the teaching team would meet each day to reflect on the learning that occurred that day and then discuss ways to extend and build on that learning in a way that is meaningful to children.

You may be wondering why daily planning is so critical to emergent curriculum and the nature-based approach. In fact, I've heard some argue that the same seasonal events occur each year, so it makes sense to just teach those things. My response is quite simply, yes, of course there are recurring seasonal events from year to year. Additionally, with children spending so much time outdoors, their ideas and interests are likely going to be based on seasonal events. However, the questions they are asking, the observations they are making, and the connections to other parts of their lives will vary from year to year. Every child arrives to your program with a wealth of experiences, and those experiences will shape how each child experiences and makes sense of the natural world. By observing and listening to children, we can provide customized experiences that leverage the natural seasonal events that are meaningful to the children in our program on any given day.

Mix Learning *in*, *about*, and *with* Nature

An NBP provides opportunities for learning *in*, *about*, and *with* nature. The balance among these three types of learning involves delicate pedagogical decisions. To address all developmental domains, all three approaches must be present to some degree.

> Teneshia and her teacher walked toward the big oak tree. Teneshia said, "Tree. *Tree* starts with *T*."
>
> "Yes," Miss Carter replied. "*Tree* starts with *T*."
>
> Just then, a deer ran across the path in front of them and disappeared into the underbrush. Teneshia excitedly beckoned to her friend Becca. "Did you see that? Did you see that deer? It ran really fast on its four legs. Deer have brown fur and white tails."
>
> Together with their teacher, the two girls headed toward the oak tree, where they each made crayon rubbings of the bark on pieces of paper. As they worked, they talked about the deer and wondered where it might be heading. They decided that it must be scared of them and was going to look for its friends.

In this example, the child is developing her oral language and emerging literacy skills related to the tree; she is learning *in* nature. At the same time, suddenly seeing the deer and describing the event to a peer is an example of learning *with* nature. The children's exploration of the tree is part of their learning both *about* and *with* nature. As a result of the integration of learning *in*, *about*, and *with*, all developmental domains are addressed. As much as possible, a nature-based approach emphasizes learning *with* over the other two approaches, but if we are truly addressing the whole child, it's impossible to ignore learning *in* and *about* nature.

It's important to reflect on the frequency of certain types of activities in your program and develop a clear understanding of the differences among these three types of learning. Learning *in* means any learning that occurs in the natural world but does not depend on nature for the learning to occur. Simply put, the learning activity would function the same way if it occurred indoors. Taking puzzles from the indoor classroom to the beyond is an example of learning *in*, because nothing about putting a puzzle together is connected to or requires the natural environment. In contrast, learning *about* nature means the content of the activity focuses on the natural world and, as with learning *in*, does not necessarily need the presence of nature to occur. Completing a puzzle that depicts an insect's life cycle would be a simple learning *about* activity. A more involved learning *about* activity might be to read a story, sing a song, or act out a play about insects.

Learning *with*, on the other hand, requires being in the physical presence of the natural environment and making a cognitive or social-emotional connection with the child. Visiting a meadow and discovering the world of insects by collecting and observing them would be an example of learning *with* nature. Now, even this moment can quickly slip back into learning *about* nature if the teacher stops the group to provide information about a particular insect. This is not to say that it's inappropriate to share information, but those moments need to be handled judiciously. By stopping to present information in a direct, didactic way, we may be supporting development of content knowledge, but if we teach in this way too often, we may also be squelching the wonder and enthusiasm for learning—part of social-emotional development. We may also be squelching opportunities for children to practice scientific observation and to ask questions that we might not have planned for. The goal is to facilitate learning *with* as much as possible, and learning *in* and *about* will not be absent.

In addition to supporting all development domains, another reason to balance learning *in*, *about*, and *with* nature is that sometimes we as adults know about interesting natural phenomena that children might not discover on their own. Maple-syrup season in the northeastern part of the United States and southeastern Canada is a great example. Children

are not going to discover on their own that the sap that flows out of a maple tree in the springtime can be boiled to become a sweet, tasty syrup. However, that is something adults know and can share.

That being said, a teacher-initiated learning *about* activity does not mean child-led learning within the activity is thrown out the window—they still take the lead after you've initiated. The pedagogy can and should still emphasize play and discovery rather than a didactic "teaching about" approach. The children, for example, might decide to pour the sap they've gathered into multiple containers rather than one. Or they might use a variety of loose parts to create their own replica of the maple tree they visited on their hike.

In-the-Moment Adjustments

Teaching is an art of constantly reacting and adjusting plans based on the needs and interests of children. This is essentially a pedagogical dance, as teachers balance who is taking the lead at a given moment, the teacher or the child. Children should lead most of the time, but occasionally teachers need to provide a question or idea to enhance the dance of learning. This responsive teaching, which responds to children's interests, experiences, and current development, has been called *improvisation* by researchers Elizabeth Graue, Kristin Whyte, and Anne Karabon. They explain:

> Teachers improvise when they actively respond to children's diverse intellectual, social, and emotional experiences and needs; taking multiple bodies of knowledge into moment-to-moment interactions with children. Teachers create individually tailored learning experiences when they use their knowledge of children inside and outside the classroom as a source for teaching.

These moment-to-moment interactions, which are individualized for each child, are important in any early childhood setting, but they are particularly important in the outdoor settings within a nature-based approach. The natural world will provide a myriad of potential learning opportunities. The art of teaching in a nature-based setting is deciding which opportunities to grab on to and which to let pass by. This decision takes into account children's experiences and needs and the natural phenomenon itself. Sometimes the natural world presents learning opportunities that will linger for long periods of time, such as leaves changing colors in the fall, and other times the opportunities might be fleeting moments, such as a bird sitting on a branch a few feet away. Is the event typical or unusual? Will this opportunity happen quickly, or will we be able to watch for an extended period of time? What other experiences have children had related to this one? Is there something children should notice now so they can make sense of it later? If it's a bird, for example, is it important for them to notice its size and colors?

There is no "right" answer to these questions. Different responses could lead to different meaningful learning outcomes. The pedagogical dance and improvisation in teaching are hard work, but the art of teaching is based on the development of skills as a teacher. The more we practice the skills of teaching, the easier it is to perform the dance and improvise in the moment. Being willing to abandon plans and embrace opportunities as they arise will support rich, meaningful learning in your nature-based program. Every day, the natural world will provide opportunities for adjusting your plans, and most of the time these moments will be much more powerful than any activity originally planned.

Becoming an NBP: A Snowy Schedule Change

DeShaun and Mike had planned for today's excursion to the beyond to involve a forest hike, giving the children a chance to explore how the trees had changed during the transition to winter. But as the group started down the trail, snow began to fall. The children began excitedly pointing at the sky as they chattered about the snow.

Seeing this development, DeShaun and Mike quickly consulted each other and decided to adjust their plans to capitalize on this new interest. DeShaun said to the children, "Check this out, everyone! Come stand by me." As the children gathered, he and Mike counted them to make sure that everyone was present. Then DeShaun continued, "Now, hold one hand up like this and catch some snowflakes!"

As the flakes landed on the children's mittens, Mike passed out magnifying glasses from his trail bag. He handed the last one to Josefina and watched as she peered through it at her snowflakes. "What do you notice about that snowflake?" he asked, pointing to one.

"It has spikes," Josefina said.

"Wow. How many spikes does it have?"

Documenting Children's Learning

An important part of any early childhood curriculum is documentation and ongoing, authentic assessment of children's learning. There are a variety of approaches available for documentation, but whatever you choose should record children's learning for later use in planning, communicating with families about children's development, and revisiting learning experiences with children. It is also important that your approach to documentation be aligned with the nature-based philosophy. This means it should include the competent voices of children. It should honor play-based learning and be rooted in observation rather than in formal assessments such as worksheets or tests. The documentation should also be a tool for building on and extending children's learning. One system that does these things, for example, is Claire Warden's Talking and Thinking Floorbooks approach, which is commonly used in nature-based settings. Whatever documentation system you choose, make sure you are recording children's ongoing learning. Then use this information to inform your daily planning. Documentation is a cyclical process, and planning cannot be done without it.

Using Other Curricula with a Nature-Based Approach

There is more and more talk about combining the nature-based approach and other early childhood curricula, such as Montessori, Waldorf, High Scope, or the Creative Curriculum. Some people insist that

established curricula and a nature-based approach cannot function effectively together. While this may be true for some curricula, most of the commonly used early childhood curricula can, with minimal effort, be aligned with the nature-based approach. Most well-known curricula outline physical environment, structure of the day, and teacher-child interactions, much as I've done in this book. If you are already using a curriculum in your program, look through it and ask yourself honestly whether those elements can be done with the nature-based approach in mind. Ask yourself, for example, if large-group meetings are a requirement, does the curriculum specify length of time and what that large-group time might look like? My guess is that it does answer those questions but does not say that the meeting must happen indoors. What if that meeting happened on the excursion to the beyond?

To summarize, do not abandon a nature-based approach simply because you have an existing curriculum. I know of several high-quality nature-based programs that implement commercially available, well-established curricula with fidelity. I suggest that you critically analyze the role of the teacher and the child in your curriculum and decide whether that aligns with the philosophical underpinnings of a nature-based approach. Some curricula, for example, do not align well with the child-centered, emergent-curriculum idea, which is important for a nature-based approach.

Ask yourself these questions to evaluate your pedagogy:

- Who does most of the talking in the classroom—teachers or children? Does this vary among the various learning spaces?

- How much do teachers interact with children in each learning space?

- How do teachers interact with the children? How do they support learning?

- Are teachers positioned as co-learners alongside children?

- How much agency or decision-making power do children have?

Next Steps

Once you have identified the gaps in your current practices and your desired practices, take the time to articulate your vision in writing. Revisit your program mission statement and philosophy statement, and ask yourself whether your vision truly reflects your purpose. If they do not align, revise them with your staff and board.

Finally, as you're making shifts in practice, it is important to write down and display the goals for implementing the nature-based approach. If, for example, you decide you want to convert your playground to a natural play area within three years, that decision should be documented for your staff. Then, of course, once it's documented, it also needs to be lived. Living the mission, philosophy, and goals is what makes the dream a reality.

Frequently Asked Questions

1. **Do I really need a written program philosophy or pedagogy statement?** Technically, no, you do not need to write these things down. However, written or not, they affect how you operate. Writing down your philosophy and pedagogy serves a few purposes. It can clarify your own thinking about how young children should be taught. It also helps clarify thinking within a team of educators. Written statements are informative both for potential and new employees and for teams who have been working together for a long time. It is an opportunity to say, "Oh, yes, that is why we do that." Written statements also inform potential and current families about why and how you operate.

2. **If we already have a program philosophy statement, do we need a new one specific to the nature-based approach?** The answer to this question depends on how different your current philosophy statement is from where you are headed. In other words, if you are planning to make significant shifts in your practice that may not fully align with your current philosophy statement, then you may want to revise the statement. If, on the other hand, you are making minor changes in practice that still align with your existing philosophy statement, you may not need to revisit it. Remember, the goal of the philosophy statement is to describe the values that underpin your policies and daily practices. If you are deviating from the values you have previously described, then yes, you should revise your philosophy statement.

Reflections on Practice

1. What is the purpose of the nature-based approach to my program? Why do I want to integrate a nature-based approach? Has that desire been documented?

2. If nature is core to my program's purpose, is that reflected in my organization's mission statement?

3. Do we have a written philosophy statement that captures all the philosophy components discussed in this chapter?

Chapter 3:
STAFFING CONSIDERATIONS

The success of the implementation of the nature-based approach is dependent on high-quality teachers effectively supported by equally high-quality administrators. While these two elements are not the only things necessary for a preschool's overall success, success cannot happen without them.

A primary goal of an NBP is to teach children to responsibly care for the natural world, and a successful nature-based program is dependent on the teachers. The physical environment and structure of the day could be ideal for a nature-based approach, but without a teacher with the right skills and attitudes, the approach will fall short. The teacher is pivotal for bringing the nature-based approach to life. This means hiring the right people and providing the necessary professional development.

All teaching requires a variety of knowledge and skills to be successful. In particular, a nature-based teacher must have the following attributes:

- The attitude of a co-learner with the children, which will be demonstrated in her interactions with them
- General content knowledge, such as reading and math, and an understanding of developmentally appropriate practice
- A strong knowledge of the natural world in that particular school's geographic setting

The next few sections discuss specifics about these broad categories of knowledge and skills.

Attitudes toward Nature-Based Learning

The most important factor in a successful nature-based program is the teacher, and the most important factor within the teacher is her attitude toward the nature-based approach. For a teacher to be successful, she must buy in to the overall philosophy and demonstrate personal attitudes and approaches to learning that support the implementation of that philosophy.

Passion

First, in terms of the overall philosophy, teachers must believe that nature is a powerful, meaningful teacher in and of itself that is necessary for children's overall development. They must also believe that children are capable, competent individuals with ideas worthy of being heard. As such, NBP teachers must believe that the best curriculum emerges out of children's experiences and ideas. The best teacher will not only believe in the nature-based approach but also exhibit a passion for teaching young children in this way.

Second, great nature-based teachers demonstrate personal attitudes and approaches to their own learning that support the overall philosophy. While it is important to believe in the teaching power of the natural world, a personal connection to the natural world is ideal. Ideally, nature-based teachers have their own intellectual, emotional, and spiritual connection to the natural world that makes them joyful to be outside every day. The ideal teacher is one who says, "Wow! Cool! What is that?" "Oh, it's beautiful!" and "I love being outside." A teacher who dreads going outside, getting dirty, being wet, being outside in winter, and so forth is probably not the best person for this job. That said, the particular activities teachers enjoy outdoors will vary widely, which is actually a positive thing within a team; a variety of experiences makes for richer social experiences and opportunities for extending learning. In the end, what matters is that the teacher has a passion for being outdoors.

A teacher must not only be passionate but also have a desire to share that passion with others. Hopefully a teacher will be able to communicate about and advocate for the benefits of the nature-based approach to young children's overall development. This communication is vital for working with parents but also helpful when working with other early childhood professionals. A good teacher can explain the learning that is occurring in her particular setting.

Weather and Dressing for Success

Another aspect of being a happy teacher outdoors is being positive about the weather conditions. Yes, there are days when it will be cold or rainy, but if the teacher and children are dressed appropriately, they will be warm and happy under their gear. Teachers should always wear appropriate clothing for the weather conditions. This keeps their focus on teaching rather than on personal physical comfort and sends a message to children and parents about what *appropriate clothing* means.

Some of you may now be wondering, "What is appropriate clothing?" Well, it depends, of course, on the weather and climate, but generally speaking, clothing is appropriate if it keeps you dry, helps you maintain a comfortable body temperature, helps protect the skin against sun damage, and keeps out any wind. Appropriate clothing can get dirty. It also allows you enough freedom of movement to run, jump, bend, and so on. Appropriate footwear will keep your feet comfortable and dry, and it should protect your ankles if you will be moving over uneven ground. Again, exact footwear depends on temperature and terrain and may mean light hiking boots, heavy winter boots, or even tennis shoes.

Personal Fears

A teacher happy to be outdoors and in nature does not necessarily enjoy *all* things about the natural world. In fact, there are very few people in the world with zero fears or dislikes about nature. Some people, for example, dislike snakes. Others are not fans of small rodents such as mice. Recognizing that we all have fears, the critical trait in a nature-based teacher is how she responds to moments of fear outdoors.

Fears are emotional reactions to things we think might harm us. *Hazards* are organisms or actions that actually could harm us. *Risk* is the likelihood of that hazard actually harming us. Most of the time, even if a hazard or risk is present, our fears are greatly out of proportion to the actual danger. When working with children, the ideal teacher is able to recognize irrational fears she is experiencing and control them. Appropriate responses might include getting quiet, calling for a coworker, or simply walking away, rather than squealing, screaming, or jumping up and down. It is important to acknowledge the emotions we feel, but this must be done in a calm, reasonable, rational manner.

Why am I making such a big deal about responding to fears? It is quite simple. The nature-based approach is designed to support children's relationships with the natural world. We do not want to put our irrational, adult fears on children. They have the right to determine for themselves what they do and do not like. If we put our fears on them, we've potentially robbed them of the opportunity to discover an amazing element of the natural world. Snakes, for example, are really amazing animals. Different species have different personalities. Anyone who's ever spent much time around me knows I'm a big fan of the beautiful black rat snake—a calm, gentle, beautiful snake. If I had seen an adult scream and flail around snakes when I was a child, I never would have learned of my love for this snake. Instead I witnessed adults who saw the wonder and beauty in snakes and knew how to handle them safely.

Teacher-Child Interactions

While overall attitude about the nature-based approach is foundational to a successful teacher, it is not the whole picture. A quality teacher demonstrates an understanding of asking open-ended questions, eliciting and extending children's ideas, addressing children's physical and emotional needs, helping children resolve conflicts, and providing direct and meaningful feedback to children. There are so many aspects of teacher-child interactions to consider—too many to discuss here. For the purposes of this book, we focus on the teacher-child interactions that are vital for effective implementation of the nature-based approach.

At the core of the nature-based approach is the belief that young children are capable individuals, a perspective that differs greatly from viewing them as dependent on adults for all aspects of their care. This belief manifests in teaching practice in a variety of ways, including emphasizing play and discovery over didactic instruction, being an active participant in that play and discovery, listening to children's voices in planning and decision-making, and having an attitude of yes.

Emphasizing and Joining in Play

Seeing children as capable means valuing their experiences and ideas in their learning, which is why supporting play and discovery demonstrates a belief in young children's abilities. As children play, they are making meaning of the world around them. Our role as adults is to help scaffold this meaning making, without spending all our time telling children the answers through direct instruction. This is not to say we never tell children things we as adults have come to know, but we are careful to tell only when children are ready to use and make sense of that information.

One way for teachers to support play and discovery is to be an active participant in the play. A high-quality nature-based teacher has a zest for life and learning. Her behavior and language conveys a personal desire to learn and discover all of the wonders of the world. Genuine use of phrases such as, "I wonder," "Let's find out," and "What do you think?" acknowledges that adults do not know everything and have a desire to learn. Additionally, teachers can model inquiry by asking children and processing aloud why and how questions. Another way to model a desire to learn and to make sense of the world is to encourage experimentation and discovery. "What do you think will happen if…" followed by, "Let's try it!" is a common exchange with an adult that not only supports but encourages experimentation.

Being an active participant in play allows for co-construction of knowledge with children while modeling positive approaches to learning. Children will see through the teacher's example that learning is fun, interesting, and an ongoing, lifelong process—just because we are adults does not mean we know everything.

Listening to Children for Planning

Yet another way for teachers to demonstrate their belief that children are capable is to listen to children's voices when planning and making curricular decisions. Sometimes people talk about "giving children a voice" in planning, but I want to be clear here. Children already have a voice. They have thoughts and ideas about their world. Our job as quality nature-based teachers is to provide them with the opportunity to have their voices heard. Our job is to listen to children and respond accordingly. A quality nature-based teacher does this daily.

An Attitude of Yes

Nature-based teachers demonstrate a belief in children's abilities by having an attitude of yes. Many times, adults' first reaction when a child asks to do something is to say no. This response typically has one of two root motivators—inconvenience or safety. Imagine, for example, that a child asks to get out paint to make a mural, and the teacher says no. What was the motivator for that response? Mostly likely, it was a thought by the adult: "Ugh. Not the paints—I don't want to have to deal with the cleanup." There are times when saying yes might not be appropriate, such as when a child asks to take out the paints five minutes before the transition to snack, but most of the time a yes is the appropriate response. The fact of the matter is, preschool children make messes. That's part of the joy of childhood. Yet most children do not have the opportunity for large-scale messes at home. For this reason, high-quality teachers must support and even encourage this joy when children are in their care. So embrace the yes, make a mess, and flourish in the joy, discoveries, and learning that occur as a result.

Now, I know there are people out there saying, "But children need to hear the word *no* sometimes." Absolutely! There are times when no is necessary for children's safety—particularly when danger is imminent and we need to stop a behavior immediately. In many safety situations, however, a pause in the action followed by a conversation with the child to talk through the safety issues is more appropriate than an immediate no. In a nature-based setting, for example, there is a lot of daily management around clothing. I have heard teachers who are just starting their nature-based journey complain that some children do not want to put on their coats when preparing to go outside. This is a moment to stop and reflect, "Is it necessary that my response be, 'No, that is not a choice right now'?" Unless the temperatures outside are extremely dangerous or the child has physical limitations that inhibit his ability to identify his own bodily needs, why not allow the child to make the choice? Having a conversation about the temperature outside and knowing that the child might change his mind, a wise teacher might simply suggest taking the coat along "just in case." This values children's abilities to make decisions about their own bodies. It also helps teach *why* we wear different clothing outside. There's nothing wrong with feeling the cold, realizing it's more comfortable to be warm, and then making the connection that we can adjust our clothing to make ourselves comfortable. In fact, this is an example of the power of nature-based education in action—immediate cause and effect, feeling fully alive, and then taking care of our own needs. In case there is confusion here, let me clarify: I am not suggesting that adults ignore the safety needs of children. I am suggesting that we support children in being agents and decision makers in their own safety.

I am by no means suggesting that we ban *no* from our vocabularies. In fact, I believe it is a powerful word that children need to hear and use to keep themselves and each other safe. However, if we are to maintain the power of the word *no*, we need to use it sparingly and when we really mean it—not when we're simply being lazy or inconvenienced. A teacher who truly values young children and their abilities will take a second or two to pause and reflect before responding to children's requests. This teacher will ask himself, "Is this really a problem, or am I making this decision for my own ease and comfort?"

Ecological Knowledge and Outdoor Skills

Content knowledge of any kind, whether literacy, science, or math, is core to quality teaching. In a nature-based setting, there is the additional content related to the local natural world. First, it's not only okay but necessary to acknowledge it is impossible to know everything about the natural world in your area. That being said, knowing the basics and constantly adding to that knowledge will contribute immensely to the quality of your teaching. Knowledge of the local natural world informs materials selection, enhances inquiry-based conversations with children, and allows for moment-to-moment adjustments. Additionally, teachers who have basic outdoor skills will help create a more positive experience for everyone. Knowledge of the natural world will help in keeping plants and animals safe from children, and vice versa, which leads us to the fact that nature-based teachers must also have knowledge of and skills related to the inherent hazards and risks in the outdoors. They must not only be able to distinguish among hazards, risks, and fears, but they must know what to do in that moment to provide a safe, meaningful learning opportunity for children.

Basic Knowledge of Local Natural History

First and foremost, nature-based teachers should have basic knowledge of natural history—the study of organisms through observation over time—in their local area. This, of course, means naming organisms. In her book *The Goodness of Rain*, Ann Pelo argues, "The Earth is not an anonymous place. . . . The absence of

"The Earth is not an anonymous place. . . . The absence of names becomes a barrier to intimacy: a bird is a bird is any bird, not this cliff sparrow, not this crag martin. When we don't know what we see, who we hear, where we walk, we don't know, really, where we are. Names are integral to relationship."

—Ann Pelo, *The Goodness of Rain*

names becomes a barrier to intimacy: a bird is a bird is any bird, not this cliff sparrow, not this crag martin. When we don't know what we see, who we hear, where we walk, we don't know, really, where we are. Names are integral to relationship."

Naming organisms brings us closer to the natural world not only in a cognitive way but also, even more importantly, in a social-emotional way. An enthusiastic nature-based teacher will know whether organisms are common or rare, where they are normally found, what their typical behavior is, and how they interact with other organisms. Part of this natural-history knowledge is also *phenology*, or the study of seasonal occurrences in your area related to climate, plants, animals, and so forth. Knowledge of individual organisms and the seasonal happenings gives you one more tool in your teaching toolbox to maximize the emergent curriculum and teachable moments. Many programs in the northern parts of the United States, for example, include a butterfly unit in the spring. Yet there are very few butterflies out and about in the spring compared to the fall. As a result, I have seen several programs move their butterfly units to the fall. The children then have many more opportunities to see a diverse range of butterfly species up close.

Knowledge of local natural history will help you support children's observations and make connections among different experiences they've had throughout the school year. For example, knowing the names of local bird and tree species enables you to help the children create links among their observations of these organisms. Which birds roost in which trees? Why might they prefer those trees over others?

A teacher's personal knowledge of the natural world can also support children's language development. Knowing and using real, scientific words provides children with a greater array of vocabulary exposure.

A great example is knowing the difference between *poisonous* and *venomous*. *Poisonous* describes something that can cause illness or death when we eat or drink it; a plant may be poisonous. *Venomous* describes an organism that is capable of injecting or transmitting a poisonous substance that can cause illness or death; a black widow spider is venomous. This new vocabulary, like all vocabulary, needs to be used in context so children understand the meaning. If you know the language, you are more likely to use it appropriately with children—thus supporting children's overall language and literacy development.

I want to share a bit of caution in having strong natural-history knowledge. Having extensive knowledge of the natural world can generate a desire to share that knowledge in a rapid-fire approach with young children. It's imperative that teachers avoid this. You want to support children's learning *about* nature, but you primarily want to support children's learning *with* nature. There will be times when it is appropriate to name an organism or provide a fact about it. The trick, however, is ensuring that children are ready and receptive for this direct telling of information. Sometimes, for example, children will directly ask, "What is that bird?" In those cases, I usually answer directly and offer observations about that bird that led me to know the answer. For example, "Oh, that's a downy woodpecker! I can tell because of the black and white markings, and it's smaller than other woodpeckers we see here." If a child is watching the bird but does not ask, I could take a few different approaches. I might have a moment of reverence and simply whisper, "Oh, wow, look at that downy woodpecker hopping around that tree." Another approach might be to support the child in making careful observations of the bird to distinguish it from other species and then perhaps put a name to it. Of course, this is not really unique to natural-history teaching. In all content areas, teachers have to decide how to elicit and extend children's content knowledge.

At this point you may now be a bit overwhelmed about all of the things you need to know, and you are not alone. Often when I suggest to teachers that they learn about the natural history of their area, they look at me with a bit of panic because there is so much to know. True, there's more to know about the natural world than one could possibly learn in a lifetime. It is possible, however, to learn enough to support children's meaningful learning. It is also possible to actively strive to continually add to your existing knowledge. In the meantime, when a child has a question that you're unable to answer, there is a simple response: "I don't know." If you're fully embracing the idea of being a co-learner, the full response would be something like, "I don't know. Let's find out! How do you think we could find out?" followed by referencing informational texts in your classroom or making intentional use of a brief online search. By admitting that you do not know but want to find out, you're positioning yourself as a co-learner rather than an all-knowing adult. This type of response demonstrates a love for lifelong learning and develops children's ability to seek and evaluate information. It also keeps your own sense of wonder alive and well.

Understanding of Risks and Hazards

Another component of natural-history knowledge is the ability to distinguish legitimate outdoor hazards and risks from fears. I discussed earlier the importance of not putting our own personal fears on children, and part of that practice is being able to identify what is a risk and what is not. There is an urban legend, in my experience particularly among adolescent boys, that the daddy longlegs (also called the harvestman) is the most venomous spider ever but that its mouthpart is not big enough to bite humans. This is false. In fact, harvestmen do not have venom glands. Knowing this can help prevent a moment of panic. These urban legends seem to be rampant when it comes to the natural world, so it's helpful to know the facts.

Of course, there *are* things in the natural world that can be harmful to us, and it's important to know what they are. In northern Michigan, where I live, there is very little to be genuinely concerned about. We have one venomous snake in our state, the eastern massasauga rattlesnake, that is very rare, timid, and typically only found in a specific kind of wetland called a *fen*. If I'm taking children to areas where that snake is found, I'll conduct a benefit-risk assessment and adjust our behavior accordingly. In the southern and western parts of the United States or in other parts of the world, however, there are greater concerns around venomous snakes and other organisms, which require not only benefit-risk assessments but also clear policies around entering their habitats.

I'm not sharing these details to pick on snakes— I really like snakes, after all—but to point out that knowing the facts about local natural history

> ## Becoming an NBP: Reacting to an Unexpected Hazard
>
> As they continued their investigation of the pond area, teacher Julie and three of the children approached a log where a snapping turtle was sunning itself. A small movement caught Julie's eye. Glancing over, she recognized a copperhead lying in the grass on the other side of the log.
>
> Julie calmly said, "Everyone, freeze." Having practiced for this very moment, the children froze in their tracks and looked at their teacher. "Slowly, and quietly as mice, move away from the log with me."
>
> When Julie and the children had moved a safe distance from the copperhead, she pointed it out to the children and talked with them about what kind of snake it was. They remarked on its coloring and how difficult it was to see among the leaves, sticks, and grass. They talked about the importance of not disturbing a wild creature. Then they walked over to another part of the shore. As she passed her co-teacher, Julie mentioned the copperhead to him, and they agreed to keep the children a safe distance from that area.

is crucial to a nature-based educator's toolbox. This knowledge supports curriculum and teacher-child interactions and is a crucial component to keeping children safe outdoors. There will still be times when we have emotional responses, but the facts can bring us back to reality quickly. The goal is to move away from what environmental educators call *biophobia*, or fear of the natural world. Ultimately, the underlying philosophy and premise of a nature-based approach is to support the children's innate human need for connection to the natural world, or *biophilia*.

Risk Management

Risk management is a significant aspect of any nature-based program. The teacher is the key to appropriate risk management. There should be clear policies and procedures in place to assist in managing risk, and it is the teachers who will implement those policies and procedures. It is also the teachers who will engage children in teacher-child interactions specifically related to risk management. We discuss risk management in more detail in the next chapter.

Understanding Rules for Handling and Collecting Organisms

Another important aspect of local natural-history knowledge is knowing the rules for handling and collecting plants and animals in your state. Federal regulations protect migratory species and species listed in the Endangered Species Act. In addition, each state has specific rules for the plants and animals within its jurisdiction, including rules for handling and collecting live animals. Learn about the rules affecting your area.

- Are there protected species on your property that children should not disturb?
- What are the rules about collecting organisms?
- How long may organisms remain in your possession?
- What are the rules for handling or collecting dead animals or parts of dead animals, including feathers, bones, fur, teeth, and so on?

Protected species can be fascinating to observe but must be left undisturbed. For example, along the southeastern U.S. coast, loggerhead sea turtles come ashore to nest and lay eggs. People will come from miles around to watch the female turtles dig holes in the sand for their eggs, and then will return later to see the baby turtles crawl out and head toward the waves. Knowing this, wildlife officials cordon off areas where turtles are. People can come fairly close to observe, but they must not interfere with the turtles or their nests in any way. Are there similarly sensitive species in your area?

In many places, wildflowers offer a breathtaking display in the spring. It's tempting to pick a few to bring back to the classroom; however, this practice can be problematic. It might hurt the individual plant, harm a population of a rare species, or disperse seeds of non-native or invasive species. Generally, it's best to stick to picking non-native species that are not extremely invasive, meaning that they do not overcrowd native species. Dandelions, for example, are a reasonable flower to pick because they're very common, not native, and do not pose a great danger to native ecosystems, but I generally discourage any other flower picking.

Generally speaking, most states allow you to have parts of animals that are considered game species, such as deer, ducks, or certain species of fish. I can confidently tell you that parts of birds of prey are not allowed without special permits. You'll need to check with your state or province to determine what is and is not allowed.

The local state or provincial department of natural resources, sometimes called the department of conservation or something similar, will be able to provide guidance. Remember, these organizations will likely

be supportive of your goals—after all, they want children experiencing the outdoors as well. Of course, they also have a duty to adhere to legislation and protect natural resources, but they are not your adversaries. They will want to work with you and will want you to work with them. Reaching out to them may even bring some really wonderful partnerships—you never know!

In summary, knowing the rules for plant and animal handling and collection in your area and being transparent about the rules with both children and families is yet another way to model environmental stewardship in a nature-based approach.

Proficiency in Outdoor-Related Skills

Last, but far from least, nature-based educators need strong outdoor-related skills. These skills include first aid, fire-building, knot tying, whittling, orienteering skills, handling of animals, weaving baskets, animal tracking, and so forth. There are so many skills related to safety, survival, arts and crafts, and natural history, and any one of these skills in a nature-based teacher's toolbox will make for a richer experience for both children and adults. For example, in terms of handling animals, once you know what you are legally able to do, it's important to know how to handle animals in a way that is safe for children and the critter. This varies by organism, of course. Amphibians, for example, are very sensitive to lotions and repellants and also need to have moist skin at all times to aid in their breathing. Thus, when handling frogs, salamanders, or other amphibians, you should wash your hands of all human-made lotions and sprays and wet your hands before handling the creature.

While many outdoor skills are needed regardless of your geographic location, there are some skills that vary depending on your setting and the typical activities associated with that setting. Cross-country skiing or snowshoeing (and the skills to assess risk in these activities), for example, might be appropriate if you live in an area with heavy winter snowfall. An educator taking children to an ocean beach, on the other hand, needs a strong working knowledge of tides and ocean currents and other water-related safety skills. No matter your location, outdoor skills are essentially another content area in a teacher's catalog of knowledge and abilities. Adults who have strong content knowledge will be able to safely and appropriately support and extend children's learning.

Administrator Support Is Key to Starting Your Program

A great nature-based program is dependent on great teachers, and great teachers are dependent on supportive, effective administrators. Administrators need to select the right teachers for the job, be clear in policies and procedures, and provide the necessary resources to implement those policies.

As I've said, the teacher is what makes or breaks the success of any NBP classroom. Thus, it's key for administrators to identify the best person for the job. I've outlined some characteristics that can be foundational in the hiring process. However, most programs wanting to implement a nature-based approach are not hiring new staff; rather, they are making an internal shift toward the approach. This means identifying and selecting current employees who will give the new approach genuine effort and a fair shot at success. The best person for the job is the one who meets the characteristics I described earlier in this chapter and, perhaps most importantly, exhibits the most passion for the approach. Mandating or forcing a teacher to implement a nature-based approach is a good way to see the project fail. Selecting a teacher who has a dislike of cold temperatures, mud, and "bugs" will not lead to success. He will likely spend minimal time outdoors, which results in a lack of fidelity to the approach. A teacher with a disdain for nature will also likely exhibit that negativity to the children. A teacher with a passion for the approach will strive daily to implement teaching practices that are true to the nature-based approach with a constant desire to be better than yesterday.

Once the right teachers have been identified, it's important to be clear about the philosophy, policies, and procedures they must follow. Your program philosophy will, of course, guide the policies and procedures.

Policies and procedures will include all of the traditional preschool policies, such as requirements for pickup and drop-off, policies regarding illness, rules around foods, and so on, and they should also include those things unique to the nature-based approach at your particular site. These policies include safety procedures related to weather emergencies, excursions into the beyond, and risky play, such as stick play and tree climbing. Once those policies and procedures are in place, it is essential that all staff members are knowledgeable of the policies and procedures. We discuss developing policies and procedures in more depth in chapter 4.

While the information about philosophy, policies, and procedures should be kept readily available in your policies and procedures manual, it should also be discussed regularly as a staff in both formal and informal ways. There should be regular formal review of all policies and procedures to remind staff of expectations and reevaluate whether those policies and procedures are still the best approach. These formal review sessions will be informed by ongoing informal conversations about the policies and procedures. These will range from comments such as "Don't forget that we must document that a child got a splinter while playing on that log" to "I've noticed that children tripping over that step is becoming a problem. Do you think we should replace it with a slope to prevent that?" Teachers are on the front lines and understand the nuances of most problems in ways that administrators cannot fully understand without the teachers' perspectives.

Once the philosophy, policies, and procedures are clearly communicated with staff, the next step for a successful administrator is to provide teachers with the necessary resources to implement them. This includes safety resources, such as first-aid kits; means of emergency communication while in the beyond, such as cell phones and two-way radios; and access to appropriate clothing for adults and children. Beyond basic safety resources, supply and equipment resources are needed for teaching and learning. Teachers need access to materials to incorporate into the classroom indoors, outdoors, and beyond; access to computers for planning and communication with families; cameras for ongoing documentation of children's learning; and so forth.

Finally, teachers need access to ongoing professional-learning opportunities. These learning opportunities should include topics related to pedagogy and content knowledge of cognitive domains, child development including social-emotional development, content knowledge related to the natural world and outdoor skills, and nature-based approaches.

NBP EXAMPLE: Dodge Nature Preschool
Location: West St. Paul, Minnesota

The Dodge Nature Preschool program offers half-day, mixed-age sessions for children ages three to five. These sessions, with a three-to-eighteen teacher-child ratio, are two hours and forty-five minutes long and are offered in two-, three-, or five-day-per-week options. The program is situated on a 110-acre preserve in West St. Paul, Minnesota. The building, specially built to house the preschool, includes three classrooms that open immediately to the outdoors. The program is accredited by the National Association for the Education of Young Children (NAEYC).

Dodge Nature Preschool offers a variety of professional development opportunities and includes a one-day learning conference, off-site presentations, visiting experiences to observe the preschool in action, and internships for students. As another outreach effort, the staff at Dodge Nature Preschool have also written and published a book, *Four Seasons at a Nature-Based Preschool,* which is worth checking out!

Frequently Asked Questions

1. **Will the training my teachers already have (for example, from college, from state licensure programs, or in a specific curriculum) transfer to the skills needed to run an NBP?** Absolutely! At the core of the nature-based approach are, of course, principles of good early childhood education. Training in working with young children will not only transfer to the nature-based approach; it is necessary to that approach. Where your teachers may need additional training is in knowledge of local natural history, understanding of risks and hazards in your area, general outdoor skills, and similar knowledge and skills needed for the unique aspects of nature-based education.

2. **Where do I find training and support for my staff?** With the growth of nature-based education, there are more and more organizations being formed to support teachers in this approach. Certain professional associations collect information about publications, workshops, and conferences on nature-based education. Some examples of these organizations are the Natural Start Alliance (www.naturalstart.org), the Northern Illinois Nature Preschool Association (www.ninpa.org), and the International Association of Nature Pedagogy (www.naturepedagogy.com).

Reflections on Practice

1. What knowledge and skills do my staff already have that are applicable to an NBP?

2. How will I help them fill in the gaps in their knowledge and skills?

Chapter 4:
PRACTICAL CONCERNS

This chapter is intended to provide a broad view of safety and logistical concerns and information on how to establish policies and procedures to address those concerns. Later in the book, I address safety concerns related to specific physical learning environments.

Overview: Special Policies and Procedures Needed for Nature-Based Preschools

Many states do not have laws specifying what policies and procedures must be established in an NBP, but here are some areas that need special consideration in this type of preschool:

- Cleaning and maintaining equipment

- Proper teacher-child ratios

- Risk-management practices

- Amount and type of staff training

- Following state regulations and maintaining licensure in the unique circumstances of an NBP

- Health and safety concerns

Some of these areas require considerable thought and planning, so the rest of this chapter provides guidance on them.

State Regulations and Licensure

Generally speaking, NBPs are required to follow state guidelines for licensing. I recognize that in some states, preschool programs are able to operate without being licensed. Some states do not license programs that have no physical facility or that operate below a certain threshold of contact hours. For example, as mentioned earlier, forest preschools often operate without licenses. Even if a program is not required to be licensed, it should adhere to its state's regulations for preschools. After all, the role of licensing is to provide minimum standards related to safety, curriculum, and instruction—something we can all agree is important. Thus, these guidelines are still relevant in an NBP setting, and if you're already operating a preschool, they are probably quite familiar to you. What you may not be as familiar with are the regulations that specifically relate to NBP practices. You'll want to review licensing regulation for guidance related to handling of plants and animals, natural play-area development, excursions into the beyond, and academic and developmental standards for preschools in your area.

Even after reviewing the regulations, you may find yourself unsure on what is required. This is when it's important to open communication with your licensing agent. Remember, we share the goal of keeping children safe. Working with the licensing agent will ensure you are following any established rules or being intentional in documenting policies and procedures where rules might be absent. The implementation of nature-based approaches is new in most places in the country, so be patient with licensing agents as you work together to establish appropriate procedures for keeping children safe.

It's impossible to give universal advice on what is or is not allowed or what safety measures must be implemented, because every state and province is different. However, the bottom line is that you must follow the regulations for your particular location. These guidelines serve as the foundation for the creation and implementation of your policies and procedures.

Establishing Policies and Procedures

Generally speaking, at an NBP, teachers remove the environmental hazards while allowing for and supporting, in a developmentally appropriate way, beneficial risk in children's play.

Organizational policies and procedures should be established to clearly communicate to all staff what is considered a hazard in your particular setting and how those hazards are removed. To establish these policies and procedures, a thorough benefit-risk assessment should be conducted for activities and scenarios you will encounter in your program. As risk and play researchers David Ball, Tim Gill, and Bernard Spiegal explain on their "Risk-Benefit Assessment Form," benefit-risk assessment is an analysis of the reasons to conduct an activity (benefits), all possible harm that might result from engaging in that activity (hazards and risks), and the steps we can take to mitigate that harm. These procedures will vary based on your particular context (climate, geography and site logistics, proximity to medical care, and so on). Thus, I won't go through every scenario, but please know you must have safety policies and procedures in place that account for the unique activities in a nature-based approach. I was recently part of an expert panel to generate best practices for NBPs that included recommendations related to safety protocols. I strongly encourage you to refer to that document, published by the Natural Start Alliance (in press), when generating policies and procedures for nature-based experiences at your site.

These policies should focus on a variety of topics, including those typically necessary in a preschool setting. Below I highlight the topics particularly relevant or unique to the nature-based approach. Please note that this is by no means an exhaustive list and that every organizational policy must be tailored to your particular setting and situation.

Health and Safety Concerns

Safety is always a concern when working with young children. Engaging in nature-based approaches brings additional unique safety challenges, which may or may not be covered in local licensing regulations. This puts more pressure on nature-based educators to be aware of safety and logistical concerns. This includes teachers' ability to distinguish among hazards, risks, and fears, and it includes organization-wide policies and procedures to ensure children's safety.

Risk Management

Any time that humans, especially young children, are out in nature, they may encounter things that could harm them. To ensure that the children in your program have a safe, enjoyable experience, it is essential to learn how to minimize danger while maximizing learning. This balancing act is known as *risk management*. Before exploring this concept in depth, we need to define some terms.

- **Hazard:** something that could potentially damage, harm, or cause adverse health effects. In a natural-play setting, any hazards that children cannot see or control themselves (for example, poison ivy or dead, overhanging branches) need to be removed or modified for them.

- **Risk:** the probability or likelihood that someone will be hurt if exposed to a particular hazard. In a nature-based setting, high-risk situations are mitigated by removing those hazards that children cannot control themselves; establishing policies, such as wearing safety gear, to reduce the likelihood of injury; teaching children how to assess and mitigate risk themselves; and allowing children to determine whether to engage in or with a risk after conducting an assessment.

- **Fear:** an unpleasant emotion caused by the belief that someone or something is dangerous. Fears are legitimate and should always be validated. There are many times, however, where fears are irrational, such as cases in which there is minimal to no risk of harm occurring. In a nature-based setting, we patiently and kindly acknowledge fears while helping children overcome any irrational ones.

As you consider these distinctions in terms, remember that the goal is to provide meaningful opportunities for children to learn by exploring while being physically, emotionally, and cognitively safe. Taking certain risks can lead to great benefits, which I discuss more in subsequent chapters, but haphazardly allowing for risk taking can be harmful. Having intentional, well-thought-out policies around hazards and risks will create a safe environment in which children can experience beneficial risks during physical, social-emotional, and cognitive learning.

Teaching children to determine risk and safety is core to a nature-based approach. Many NBPs also engage in teaching outdoor skills such as fire building and whittling. These riskier activities are incredibly valuable for children's development and require clear procedures to ensure that children are not only safe but also learning appropriate safety measures for future application. It's important to outline policies and procedures about what risk taking is or is not allowed in the program and how those rules are communicated to staff, parents, and children. Are children allowed, for example, to climb trees? What are the protocols around such an activity? Must they, for example, climb only if they can get into and out of the tree without teacher assistance?

While there are many higher-risk activities that programs may engage in, here are a few common activities that should have clear written protocols:

- Water activities
- Tree climbing
- Fire building
- Cooking—over a fire or a gas camp stove
- Tool use—saws, hammers, knives
- Stick play
- Foraging for food

The protocols for these activities should include details on equipment needed, teacher behaviors, and children's behaviors before, during, and after the activity. The details of these protocols should, of course, be based on children's ages, number of staff involved in an activity, and any features of your particular site, such as climate, distance to emergency medical care, and so on.

Clothing and Appropriate Dress

The nature-based approach is intended to provide children with positive outdoor experiences. An essential component to making an outdoor experience positive for a child is appropriate clothing. Your program policies should outline expectations for children's clothing in different weather situations, as well as expectations for teacher and staff clothing. Too much clothing in heat can cause a child to overheat and be uncomfortable. Too little clothing in cold can also cause discomfort. The specific clothing items that you require in your program will vary depending on your climate and the time of year. The basic principle, however, of clothing selection is to help your body maintain its normal temperature at all times.

While families generally provide clothing, clothing is so important in an NBP that your program should not rely solely on parents to provide the gear. Every program implementing a nature-based approach should stock extra pieces of all types of clothing in a variety of sizes. Organizations will need to allocate money for ensuring there is appropriate clothing available, allocate space for storing these pieces of clothing, and establish procedures for managing this gear. Because children may need additional gear at any time (such as if their own gets wet), most programs find it useful to have a clothing storage space that is in a common area and is easily accessible by children, parents, and teachers. Hooks for rain gear, coats, and pants are helpful, as are baskets for gloves, mittens, and hats. Depending on the size of your program and the amount of extra gear you have, you may choose to rotate the communal gear seasonally and store the unnecessary clothing elsewhere until it is needed again.

Group Management

Group management is a challenge in any setting, but it's particularly important when leaving the natural play area to experience the beyond. Policy and procedure documents should address this issue by outlining the appropriate teacher-to-child ratios for your unique setting. What is the minimum number of adults who should be present? How does this number change as the number of children or the activities change? If, for example, you are in a more remote location or engaged in higher risk activities, you will want more adult supervision.

Additionally, there should be clear policies and procedures for managing the group—in the classroom, in the natural play area, and while on the trail. I know many programs, for example, that use an animal call to gather the children rather than yelling or whistling. Many programs have a policy of having a teacher always at the front and end of the group when hiking. How will you establish boundaries for children's play in spaces where there are no fences? For instance, taking a wagon into the beyond is not only a way to haul equipment; it can also be designated as a group meeting point or a boundary marker. Also, don't forget to include details in the policies about counting children—should this always occur during certain activities or at certain time intervals? Children should obviously be counted before departing an area, but if you're traveling along a trail with curves and areas hidden from vision, it would be wise to count more often. Particularly as programs begin to venture outside the natural play area into the beyond, group management is a critical component of your policies and procedures.

Cleanliness and Hygiene

Part of the joy and wonder of an NBP is getting messy and exploring with our hands all sorts of interesting things in the natural world. This also means we have to have clear procedures for cleanliness and hygiene. Hygiene-related policies should be established related to when it is and is not appropriate to touch natural materials, toileting procedures when exploring the beyond, consuming food from the garden, handwashing, and so forth. Again, your state's licensing regulations may not provide specific guidance on these topics, but you can use those regulations as a starting point and then work with your licensing agent to determine appropriate procedures. Handwashing, for example, is an essential practice in any preschool, but it is particularly important in an NBP. Of course, handwashing is imperative before meals and snacks. It should also be done after handling living or dead animals. Sticks are a great tool for investigating dead animals and animal scat (the scientific word for poop), and using them helps reduce the transmission of bacteria and viruses, though hands should still be washed after these investigations. Often on hikes to the beyond, there is no access to running water, so carry hand sanitizer in your trail bag to tide you over until you can get to a hand-washing station. Your written policies should describe the necessary steps for handwashing, when it is to occur, where it should take place, and so on.

Toileting in the beyond is a frequent concern for many people venturing into the nature-based approach. In most nature-based programs, toileting on the trail is limited to urgent, emergency situations. To avoid such situations, adults encourage children to use the restroom before departure, avoid venturing too far from the building, or stop the group at bathroom facilities along the trail. Again, your policies should reflect the situation at your particular site.

Of course, even with the best of precautions, emergency toileting situations in the beyond will arise with young children. So how do you handle them? Well, going to the bathroom in the woods is a good life skill, so teach children how to do it appropriately. Peeing is fairly straightforward, and your policies about it will mostly relate to location (off the trail, behind a designated tree, or whatever is appropriate for your program), privacy-related issues, and handwashing afterward. Pooping in the woods is much more complicated. The best solutions I have seen involve bringing along a camp-style potty chair, a pop-up tent for privacy, toilet paper, and water for handwashing. Programs using this approach are generally spending more than four hours away from the building. This is unusual for most preschool programs, but it is definitely something to consider if you want to venture into the beyond for longer periods of time. The main point is to consider the unique circumstances and activities at your site and create policies accordingly.

First-Aid Situations

While the goal of establishing policies and procedures for risk management is to avoid emergency situations and prevent the need for first aid, the fact is that accidents happen. The most common first-aid situations will be minor cuts and scrapes, splinters, twisted ankles, or similar injuries. Policies and procedures should be written about how to handle these situations, how the response might vary depending on location, and necessary documentation after the fact. If you're already operating a preschool, these policies will essentially be the same as your current first-aid policies. Where the details might vary is in dealing with these minor injuries while in the beyond. Ice packs, for example, are a common first-aid remedy in preschool.

Indoors, it's easy to open the freezer and grab an ice pack for a minor injury, but it would be impractical to bring a freezer with you into the beyond. Instead, you might include instant cold packs in your trail bag's first-aid kit.

Your policies should also include major first-aid scenarios in the beyond, such as allergic reactions, broken bones, cardiac episodes, and so on. While the general procedures will be the same as in your indoor policies (such as calling 911 as soon as possible), being away from the building can add an extra challenge to these emergency situations. How, for example, will you communicate your situation and location to emergency personnel? While one teacher is calling emergency responders, will another be notifying administrators? How will you handle the rest of the children while the emergency is being tended to? In addition to creating in-the-moment policies for these types of situations, you will need to create policies for generating incident reports after the fact, communicating with parents and news media about the incident, and so on.

Other Worst-Case Scenarios

Aside from injuries, there are other types of emergency situations that you must be prepared to encounter inside, outside, or beyond. First and foremost are unexpected weather emergencies. Many of these situations can be avoided by having a policy of always checking the weather prior to heading outside. There may be times, however, when a thunderstorm pops up unexpectedly or a flash flood occurs while you are in the beyond. Your policies for these situations should explain details such as where you will take the children for safety and how you will communicate to administrators back at the building.

In addition to nature-related emergencies, human-related emergency situations can also occur within your group, such as a lost child, a kidnapping, or a disgruntled parent. Most preschools have policies already written for these scenarios, but the key here is to make sure your policies address the unique challenges of being outside—particularly in the beyond space. Without doors to lock, an administrator to check identification, additional staff to help look for a child, or other resources that you would typically have for an emergency in a school building, how will you handle these scenarios in the beyond? Will you have a code system for radioing back to the building?

Additional situations to plan for are those you might encounter outside your class group. These might include encountering a large wild animal, a stray dog, or a suspicious or unusual-acting person. As I've mentioned, the exact details of the procedures will vary based on your particular context, but in most cases, they will involve calling law enforcement while moving children away from the hazard as quickly as possible.

Teaching Children about Health, Safety, and Risk Management

While it is vital that administrators and teachers are well versed in policies and procedures, children should be well-versed in these rules as well. Part of this is engaging children in ongoing conversations about safety concerns with activities in which they engage. These conversations can happen in a more formal way through a benefit-risk assessment or in more informal interactions.

Formal Benefit-Risk Assessment

Anytime children are engaging in risky play for the first time, teachers should support them in conducting a benefit-risk assessment, just as the adults have done in establishing policies and procedures. Then, with subsequent engagement in that activity, teachers can support the children in recalling the benefit-risk assessment they've already conducted. At minimum this is a conversation with children, but many programs choose to document these teacher-child conversations in writing.

For me, the essence of the conversation and documents comes down to some variation on three simple questions:

1. What are the benefits of doing this activity?

2. How might we (or nature) get hurt doing this activity?

3. How can we keep ourselves, each other, and nature safe doing this activity?

By helping children answer these three questions, we are making safety a top priority, supporting development of children's executive function skills, and providing them with agency, or control, in their own lives.

Let's say, for example, children want to dig in the dirt with real, metal shovels. They might cite benefits such as, "We can make a big pile of dirt over here!" "'Cause we can make a huuuuuuge hole!" "Because it'll be messy!" A benefit I hear a lot from children, which really is the only answer needed, is, "Because it's fun!"

The response to question 2 may include a wide range of ideas, such as getting hit in the face with the handle, hitting our feet with the shovel blade, or tossing dirt in a neighbor's eyes. For each of these answers, teachers would ask children how they could keep each other safe from these possible harms. How much direction children will need depends on their age and experience, but answers might include, "Keep space between each other so we don't get hit in the face," "Always wear shoes while shoveling in case we hit our toes. Then our toes will be safe," and "We have to look behind us before we throw dirt over our shoulders." The role of the teacher here is critical to the conversation. Are the solutions truly ones that will keep children safe? Are there other likely risks that need to be mitigated? What are reasonable ways to do so?

The beauty of these three questions is that they can be asked anywhere, anytime, and for any kind of activity. The questions are pertinent whether inside building a block tower or outside climbing trees, because they all focus on keeping ourselves, each other, and nature safe.

For ongoing, high-risk activities, these benefit-risk assessments should be completed and documented in the policies and procedures manuals. If, for example, you build fires regularly with children, the benefit-risk assessment should be formally completed and included in your policies and procedures manual, so all staff are aware of the procedures. The procedures should be communicated openly with the children, and they should have opportunities to suggest revisions to those procedures through ongoing conversations about safety.

Informal Interactions around Benefit-Risk Assessment

This idea of ongoing conversations about safety brings us to the second way teachers support risk management. This can be done through teacher-child interactions in informal, moment-to-moment interactions. This includes thinking out loud, in which teachers make their safety thinking visible to children. A teacher, for example, might say, "Before we leave on our hike, I need to count everyone to make sure we're all here." This teacher self-talk can occur in play as well: "Oh, I'm going to move this log because it's wobbly, and I'm worried I might fall." These moments are not direct, formal instruction about safety, but they model for children that safety should always be part of our thinking.

Other informal moments may include prompting a child to think about safety during play. For example, while observing a child, a teacher might say something like, "I'm concerned that rope might trip someone. What is your plan to keep everyone safe?" This opens the door for a conversation that positions the child to do the thinking rather than the teacher mandating a particular rule. This might then lead to the more formal benefit-risk assessment, or a child might provide an explanation that satisfies the teacher.

Safety and risk management should be ongoing conversations that occur both formally and informally throughout the day. This means risk management must be on teachers' minds throughout the day and an intentional part of children's language as well.

Frequently Asked Questions

1. **Children frequently get dirty during outdoor play. How can we keep the indoor classroom clean?** Sand, water, mud, dirt, snow, and slush are part of outdoor play. But if they accompany the children inside, they can create safety hazards and upset your custodial staff. To address these problems, a common policy is to have every child bring a pair of "indoor shoes" and a complete change of clothes to keep at school. After outdoor play, the children change into their clean indoor shoes (and clothes, if necessary). This practice helps keep any outdoor debris that is brought inside the classroom to a minimum. If children get totally covered in mud outside, you may want to hose them down before going indoors. After that, the children's spare clothes and a washing machine are your friends.

2. **How much is too much mud or water on a child? Or is there such a thing?** Children are washable! Seriously, though, mud, dirt, water, and so on are only problems if they cause a child to become cold or uncomfortable. Beyond this, the threshold for "too much" will be determined by individual children. Some children do not enjoy being covered in mud and thus will not pursue that option during outdoor play.

Reflections on Practice

1. What policies and procedures do we currently have in place for minor injuries? serious injuries? cleanliness and hygiene? encounters with dangerous animals or people?

2. Do these policies account for the different scenarios possible in the three learning spaces (inside, outside, and beyond)?

3. What scenarios from this chapter are not currently covered by our policies and procedures?

4. Have we thoroughly reviewed the relevant licensing regulations that might address these policies and procedures?

PART II:
PHYSICAL LEARNING ENVIRONMENT

This section of the book focuses on the inside, outside, and beyond spaces that provide the backdrop and materials for children's nature-based learning. These curricular spaces represent the philosophical underpinnings of blurring the lines between the human and natural worlds—moving closer to the idea of being interconnected with nature rather than separate from it. Therefore, the three spaces intentionally move from areas that are highly structured and human designed to an unstructured space where nature is the architect.

This section is where the rubber meets the road, or where the philosophy manifests in physical form. *Everything* in the physical environment, from laundry facilities to material choices such as children's puzzles, reflects your program philosophy. Our discussion primarily focuses on the three curricular spaces. We start indoors, then discuss the outdoor play area, and later move to the beyond.

Chapter 5:
THE INDOOR CLASSROOM

NBPs are rooted in high-quality early childhood education. As a result, there are many similarities to a traditional preschool; the indoor space is one of the most obvious. At first glance, the indoor classroom at an NBP will look like a traditional preschool, complete with blocks, art, library, dramatic play, and so on. If you look more closely at a nature-based program, however, you'll notice the entire room infused with nature. The indoor spaces at an NBP intentionally reflect the nature and culture where that program is located. The connection to outdoor materials does not stop when the children cross the building's threshold. Every element in the indoor environment is put there intentionally to serve a purpose for learning—whether related to direct instruction or classroom administration.

As much as possible, the toys, equipment, and images reflect the natural world surrounding that classroom. Ideally an NBP will have a natural feel with wood furniture and walls, lots of natural lighting, and clear views to the outdoors. Primary colors and plastic furniture are not a good fit for NBPs, as they provide an artificial look that has little do with the local environment. This effect can overwhelm the senses. Instead, the space should feel warm, welcoming, and calming.

Often, people who first visit NBPs ask whether the program is Reggio inspired. While most do not formally follow a Reggio approach, there is commonality between the approaches. A Reggio Emilia environment has a soft feel that encourages the use of the senses and provides continuity within the school and outside by supporting social relationships. Both Reggio Emilia and nature-based education believe in blurring the divide between the indoor and outdoor spaces to create a connection to place and community. This blurring of the divide allows for greater reflection of the local place. In their book on learning environments called *Rethinking the Classroom Landscape*, colleagues Sandra Duncan, Rebecca Kreth, and Jody Martin ask whether, if they blindfolded you, put you on a plane, and dropped you in a typical preschool classroom somewhere in your country, you would know where you were. I would venture that the answer to that question would most likely be a strong no. In high-quality NBPs, however, the answer would be a resounding yes. The indoor space would be reflective of the outdoor natural environment as well as the cultural environment. Attending an NBP in the hardwood forests in the upper Midwest will look and feel very different from one in the Southwestern desert. The indoor learning environment reflects not only place but also the program philosophy.

Following are some suggestions for intentionally creating an indoor environment that reflects your place and supports the overall nature-based philosophy. The indoor classroom includes two types of space:

curricular—areas where play and learning happen—and noncurricular—entries, hallways, storage, bathrooms, and so on. Both types can be used to further the mission of an NBP.

Design Principles for Curricular Spaces

When it comes to designing learning spaces for children, it's easy to become overwhelmed. After all, there are a seemingly endless number of decisions to make. What color should the walls be? How many books should be in the library? Should they be facing cover out or spine out? Which areas should be next to each other in the classroom? I could go on and on. My job here, however, is not to stress you out but to ease the burden of designing indoor spaces. For now, I want to focus on the indoor spaces that will serve as primarily play spaces for the children, the areas that support your curriculum.

In most early childhood classrooms, you will find various play or interest areas, including library, blocks, dramatic play, and art, among others. Some programs may have slightly different names for these areas, such as "house" instead of "dramatic play." Some programs have a sand and water table that is separate from the sensory table. Despite some minor differences in names and groupings of activities, the basic setup is the same. This is true even in an NBP classroom. A high-quality NBP will also include a library area, blocks, dramatic play, sensory table, toys and games, art, science discovery area, music, and cooking opportunities. It perhaps goes without saying that NBPs will bring natural outdoor materials indoors. What may not be as obvious, however, is that the indoor space is not about simply transplanting materials indoors. Materials should be meaningful to the learning that is crossing the bounds of the physical environment, indoors, outdoors, and beyond. Through my work in NBPs, I have identified a few guiding principles related to indoor curricular spaces that may help with the process.

1. Use natural instead of manufactured materials.

2. Choose authentic instead of cartoon-like.

3. Avoid stereotypes.

4. Represent nature as found in your local environment.

5. Connect the indoors to the outdoors.

6. Take advantage of science and math learning opportunities.

Use Natural Instead of Manufactured

Natural materials such as wood are always preferable to man-made materials such as plastic. On a small scale, natural materials create a different experience when the child is touching the object. Imagine picking up a scissor holder made of a piece of log rather than a plastic cup from the dollar store. The sense of touch is engaged in very different ways with these objects. On a large scale, a group of natural materials creates a feeling of calm and comfort. The natural look and feel of objects indoors reflects the same principles we're trying to accomplish outdoors—calm, mindful, with senses engaged but not overwhelmed. Nature awakens the senses but does not overwhelm them. We want to replicate this concept in the indoor space. Thus, be intentional in decorating the indoor space.

By moving toward natural materials you will also, by default, shift to more authentic materials. The most obvious change is bringing plants and animals into the classroom. (For more about animals in the preschool classroom, see the book *Connecting Animals and Children in Early Childhood* by Patty Born Selly.)

Integrating Natural Materials into the Indoor Classroom

Below are some specific examples by interest area of ways to integrate natural elements into the indoor classroom. This is by no means an exhaustive list—let your creativity be your guide!

Library
- Nature-based storybooks
- Nature-based nonfiction
- Field guides
- Maps

Dramatic Play
- Dress-up insect wings
- Stuffed animals
- Puppets
- Birding vests
- Fishing vests
- Blaze orange hunting vests and hats
- Fish and game laws for your state (for children to include in play)
- Dress-up animal hats, ears, and/or tails
- Binoculars

Blocks
- Tree blocks
- Tree bridges
- Sensory blocks with natural elements
- Animals
- Tree lacing blocks and beads
- Photos of community features on blocks
- Photos of structures children have built with loose parts outside

Games
- Animal puzzles
- Floor puzzles with animal life cycles
- Matching games with animals or insects
- Felt games, such as carrot patch letter matching

Art
- Pinecones
- Feathers
- Rocks
- Sticks
- Leaves
- Leaf and track stamps
- Leaf and track rubbing plates

Cooking
- Fruit—look for seeds
- Fruits, veggies, and herbs from garden
- Clover for class pet
- Apples or berries for sauce or jam

Writing Center
- Nature sight words, such as *bird, nest, tree, pond*

Then begin adjusting the materials within the room. You might start by replacing all your plastic cups with glass ones. Instead of using plastic bowls to hold loose parts in the art area, use baskets. Then consider adding some wooden bowls, or keep an eye out for a rock with a divot worn in the top that might serve as a bowl. With every object you bring into the classroom, ask yourself, "Is there a more natural version of this object that would serve the same purpose?"

Sensory Center

- Snow/ice
- Seeds
- Corn kernels
- Bones
- Pinecones

Science Discovery

- Furs and skulls
- Microscope
- Binoculars
- Rocks
- Tree pieces
- Seed pods
- Bird-egg replicas (or real ones!)
- Pinecones
- Feathers
- Bones
- Shells

Throughout the Room

- Houseplants
- Pets, such as rabbits, guinea pigs, fish, hissing cockroaches, and so on
- Nature as decoration
- Natural lighting
- Views to the outdoors
- Photos, materials, and so on that support the blurring of the indoor-outdoor line

Music

- Rain sticks
- Animal calls
- Hoof shakers
- Objects that make sounds similar to animal sounds (for example, running your thumb over a comb makes a sound like a chorus frog's call)
- Bird and frog calls

Choose Authentic Instead of Cartoon-Like

While the material of the object is important, the image or message being portrayed by an object is even more important. In selecting materials, it's important that we move away from cartoon-like images of nature to real ones, and it's important that we avoid reinforcing stereotypes of nature by only portraying common views of nature. Early childhood supply catalogs are full of cartoon images of the world adorned in bright primary colors. The world is not that way. Dancing bears in tutus are commonplace in catalogs, yet I've never seen a dancing bear in real life—let alone one in a tutu. Why would we provide these images for children? Children deserve to experience the world in its authentic form. NBPs see children as capable, competent individuals. Providing them with real images of the world brings that philosophy to life, demonstrating that we think they're capable of understanding and appreciating the world as it really is. In fact, we think the world is so amazing in its purest form that we want to provide children with that experience. This means the walls should not be littered with images, posters, and charts. What is displayed should be meaningful to the children—ideally created by them—and related to the learning that is happening indoors, outdoors, and beyond. Because it really can't be said too much—don't clutter the walls with junk!

Avoid Stereotypes

Part of providing an authentic learning environment for children in a nature-based setting is avoiding stereotypes of nature. For example, consider the classic *a*-is-for-*apple* letter line, on which the apple is red and there is a smiling worm coming out of it. Not all apples are red! In addition, worms do not have eyeballs or lips—how is that worm smiling? There are many other nature stereotypes that appear in early childhood classrooms. Although the monarch butterfly gets most of the attention in preschool classrooms, the North American Butterfly Association points out that there are about 20,000 butterfly species worldwide, with approximately 725 in North America alone. There are many more species of birds than cardinals, robins, and the great horned owl. Depictions of farm animals often include black-and-white-spotted cows and pink pigs. There are hundreds of domestic cattle and pig breeds. The world is full of biodiversity, and the materials in the classroom should reflect this variety. Unfortunately, many resource catalogs have bought in to the stereotypes. For example, I once bought a package of small plastic North American mammals. Among the animals was a wolf with bright red eyes. Wolves do not have red eyes! Putting this toy into the classroom would only reinforce the stereotype of wolves as scary, evil animals. (In this case, I simply took a black marker and changed the eye color.) You may have to search a little harder for appropriate toys, games, and books that represent authentic views of the natural world, but this effort will provide children with a richer experience.

Represent Nature as Found in Your Local Environment

Strive to provide materials that represent nature as found in your local environment. In many ways, this is like the avoiding stereotypes principle, but in this case, it applies on an ecosystem level. If, for example, your program is in a northern hardwood forest, the organisms from that forest should be represented in your materials—oaks, maples, white-tailed deer, barred owls, blue jays, and flying squirrels. If you live in the desert of Arizona, materials depicting different cacti, scorpions, roadrunners, coyotes, and hummingbirds would be ideal. Similarly, if you live near the ocean in the Pacific Northwest, choose materials depicting seals, sea otters, salmon, and terns.

Now, this is about the time when someone says, "But I have a child who loves dinosaurs." My response is that children's interests are always a priority. So yes, if a child is passionate about dinosaurs, then include books, toys, and games that support that interest. A teacher's job is to scaffold that interest and provide opportunities for other interests to develop as well. This means dinosaurs should not be the only animals represented in your classroom. Most of the materials should represent your local ecosystems. In addition, there may be resources available to connect the child's interest in dinosaurs with local natural resources. What dinosaurs used to live in your area? What did they look like? How do dinosaurs compare to the animals we see today? There are opportunities for comparison of other ecosystems to the ones where we live, but that comparison serves to help us better understand our own place.

Representing the local ecosystem supports blurring the lines between the indoors and the outdoors from a curricular perspective. Materials that are representative of the local environment are more likely to prompt conversations or spark play based on a memory from the outdoor experiences. This means children's learning can easily connect with their learning that occurred in another physical space. Yes, far-off ecosystems are fascinating because they're different and new, but there are also many new and interesting things to discover in our own backyards, and those things are more concrete and tangible for children. Also, the real, typical, and local representations of nature convey a message of the value of the natural world. Authentic presentation of nature shows that we see and value nature as its own entity rather than something we must change or manipulate to "make it better" or "more interesting." The natural world is incredibly interesting and meaningful as it is—without us putting tutus or bow ties on it.

Connect the Indoors to the Outdoors

Integrate nature into the indoor classroom by regularly asking, "How can the indoor space better connect to the outdoors?" Again, the idea is to blur the lines between the indoors and the outdoors so that children's learning is ongoing no matter the physical space. The physical structure of your classroom is significant in accomplishing this. If possible, provide natural light through lots of windows that are low enough so that children can see out of them. I once had a teacher explain to me that she liked her higher windowsills because the children weren't distracted by what was outside. Ack! The outdoors isn't a distraction; it is vital to helping children make sense of their world. They'll notice changes in the seasons over time. They'll notice shifts in daylight. They'll notice a bird that landed on the feeder. They'll capture moments of quiet, reflective time.

In addition to the physical structure, the materials you provide can better connect indoor and outdoor learning. There are many ways to bring this principle to life. If you have low windows with a view to the outdoors, for example, provide bird feeders where children can observe the birds and squirrels. Provide

binoculars for observing those animals and bird identification books in case children want to learn about the birds they're seeing. Also provide paper and writing utensils so they can draw what they're seeing. Have a way for the children to record how many of the different kinds of birds or squirrels they observe. I've seen this done with numbers on rings that can be flipped, dry erase boards with check marks, and an abacus with a photo of the animal on each row.

Additionally, consider how the materials you already provide for children could be enhanced to better connect indoor and outdoor learning. For example, a typical display in a preschool classroom is a number line. What if the children gathered objects outdoors, then photos of those collections became your new number line? Suddenly the display has gone from disconnected from children and the outdoors to a meaningful math and outdoor connection for the children. I visited a classroom that had a color-matching activity where children matched the color on a clothespin with a master color chart. By changing the photos on the clothespin to plants and animals in the local environment, the opportunities for conversation increased substantially. The conversation became, "I see you put the blue jay on the white spot. Can you tell me more about why you chose the white spot?" In addition, the images may elicit stories of children's recent experiences outdoors. This change in material is seemingly minor but can have a significant impact on learning.

Take Advantage of Science and Math Learning Opportunities

Now, you may be thinking, "But nature-based education is holistic and not just focused on science and math." You would be correct. I believe, however, that the nature-based approach provides excellent openings for science and math learning. Providing texts and tools that support inquiry of the natural world is simply wise use of a golden learning opportunity. There are many small shifts to the environment that can enhance children's science and math development. Real measuring tools are probably the easiest addition, and these support both science and math. Encourage children to measure the girths of different tree trunks and to notice which types of trees are larger and which are smaller. In the sensory table, rather than using recycled yogurt containers, provide children with varying sizes of beakers, graduated cylinders, and cooking measuring cups. Eyedroppers and syringes (no needles, of course) are great additions as well. These materials provide an opportunity for richer language and extension of learning: "What are those numbers on the side of that container? There are numbers on that other container also! I wonder if I pour the water from this container into that one if it will be at the same number." I'm not suggesting these conversations will happen daily, but I am suggesting that there are more opportunities for these types of conversations with real science materials.

When it comes to the indoor classroom environment, strive to integrate authentic materials and nature as much as possible. Blur the line between indoors and outdoors.

Pencils

As you're doing that, remember to keep things simple and be flexible. Don't beat yourself up if you haven't fully integrated nature into every nook and cranny of your classroom. This is an ongoing process. As I've said, even the best NBPs have improvements to make.

Design Principles for Noncurricular Spaces

Everything in your program sends a message about what is valued in your program. Obviously, classrooms themselves send the biggest message, but even nonclassroom spaces, such as entries and hallways, convey values. In a nature-based setting, you'll see nonclassroom spaces that include places to hang muddy and wet clothes, access to laundry facilities, and stashes of extra outdoor gear for any child who might need it. Those all send messages about the value placed on daily outdoor time—no matter the weather. Stores of extra clothes convey the message that the outdoor time is so valuable that you want no child to have a barrier to experiencing the outdoors. Even having laundry facilities on site shows that dirt is a typical and fully embraced part of the program.

Another value in a nature-based setting is environmental sustainability. A program that serves fresh, local food and provides recycling and composting facilities, real plates and silverware, and cloth napkins is demonstrating the importance of environmentally sustainable behaviors.

Even the photos and decorations in a program send a message about what is important. Is the artwork made by children? Are the photos of children outdoors in the mud and snow? These nonclassroom spaces are still part of your day-to-day functioning. These spaces send a message to staff, children, and parents about what is important to your program.

A Word about Technology

Technology in early childhood education is a hot topic. Typically, when people discuss technology these days, they are referring to electronic screen media. A 2010 study by the Kaiser Foundation found that children ages eight to eighteen are exposed to ten hours and forty-five minutes of screen media each

day. Each day! That is more than a full-time job! With so much exposure to screen time in daily life, I do not believe the preschool classroom should mindlessly provide screen exposure.

There is, however, a role for technology in the classroom. After all, electronic devices are tools, just like knives or shovels, and we should teach children how to use them appropriately. This means screen time should be used sparingly and with intention. For example, many nature-based programs will position a motion-sensor camera in the woods to capture images of wild animals. Viewing those photos on the computer is an appropriate use of screen time. If a child sees a bird and wants to hear the bird call, a quick internet search is a great way to scaffold his learning.

In addition to electronic media technology, it's important to remember the wide variety of other technology that children can be exposed to in the indoor and outdoor environments. Simple machines such as pulleys, wedges, screws, and levers are no-screen technologies that support children's learning. Binoculars, cameras, and microscopes support learning and help blur the lines between the indoors and outdoors. The key with selecting technology is to remember that moving toward a nature-based approach means emphasizing real, hands-on, sensory experiences as much as possible. Technology should be like any other material in the classroom—designed to enhance those experiences.

Deer-Carcass Trail Camera

Sometimes when exploring the natural world, there are signs of animals' presence even though we cannot see the creatures themselves. Technology, in the form of a motion-sensor trail camera, is a great tool for getting a glimpse of those animals when we're not around.

For example, at the Chippewa Nature Center's Nature Preschool, during a wintertime hike to the beyond, the children discovered a dead deer in the

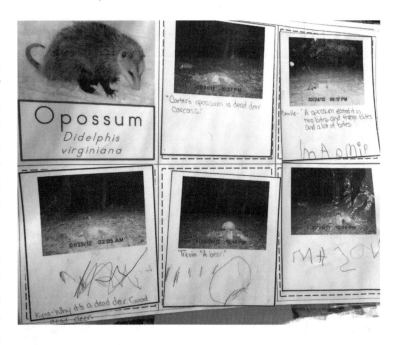

forest. Noticing tracks in the snow and curious about the animals that were visiting the deer, the group decided to place a motion-sensor trail camera on the deer. Over several weeks the children reviewed the photos from the camera, revisited the deer to see decomposition in progress, and then created a field guide to document the animals they were seeing. While this initial activity was happenstance, it was such a powerful experience that teachers and staff at the Chippewa Nature Center now place a road-killed deer in the woods each winter for the students to study.*

In the spring, children discovered a dead bird—specifically, a yellow-bellied sapsucker—on the trail. Having experienced the deer carcass and trail camera earlier in the year, they decided they

We used Merlin ID. App and followed clues about colors and size. We found out that it's a Yellow-bellied Sapsucker!

We read that boys have a red cap and throat. Our bird is a boy!

should put the bird and a camera in the woods. In preparation, they made observations and drew pictures of the bird. Once they set up the camera, photos showed that some people had walked by, a turkey and a raccoon had visited, and then a house cat had carried the bird away! The teachers later documented the experience by creating a book about the study.

*Please check your state's regulations regarding the collection of animals before moving an animal carcass.

In both examples, the intentional and purposeful use of technology allowed children to learn about food chains, decomposition, and big concepts like life and death and also gave them opportunities to practice literacy skills in the process.

Frequently Asked Questions

1. **How much technology use is too much for preschool children?** The answer to this question partly depends on how we define *technology*. If we think of technology broadly and as including items beyond electronic devices, then children should have lots of exposure to technology. If *technology* means *electronic devices*, then the answer is different. The Council on Communications and Media of the American Academy of Pediatrics recommends that children ages two through five have no more than one hour each day with screen media, and that hour should be focused on high-quality programming. When we consider children's exposure to screens outside of school, in my opinion, preschool time should not include screen media unless that media is used judiciously and intentionally.

2. **Where do I find appropriate materials for my classroom?** There are more and more companies selling nature-based materials for preschool classrooms. I have provided information about some of these companies in Appendix C. In addition to those sources, scour the pages of early childhood catalogs; every now and again you will find one or two hidden gems.

3. **Can I have a class pet that is not found in the wild in my area (such as a gerbil or a parrot)?** Absolutely! While most of the nature-based approach focuses on native, local species, a classroom pet is most often going to be an animal that is not found in the wild in your area. It's important that any pet in your classroom is there legally, so be sure to purchase your pet through a reputable pet supplier. Class pets allow children to have up-close and personal relationships with a living creature that they can care for and nurture.

4. **I have had a class pet for some time but now have a student who is allergic to it. How can I make this a positive experience for everyone?** This is the reality of a classroom with multiple children. Brainstorm creative alternatives so that a pet can be available to the rest of the children while keeping the child with allergies safe. For example, the pet could be kept in the preschool director's office, and small groups of children could leave the classroom with a teacher to care for and visit the pet.

Reflections on Practice

1. Does the indoor classroom have a general appearance of natural colors and materials?

2. Do materials primarily present authentic representations of plants and animals? In what ways could I provide more authentic representations of plants and animals? What materials could I swap out or modify?

3. Do materials represent the local environment? In what ways could I bring more of the local environment into the classroom? What materials could I swap out or modify?

4.   How can I better connect the indoor space to the outdoors?

5.   How is technology currently used in the classroom? Is this true to my philosophy of early childhood education?

6.   Do noncurricular spaces in the building support the mission of this school?

Chapter 6:

THE OUTDOOR CLASSROOM: THE NATURAL PLAY AREA

Given the emphasis on outdoor time in an NBP, it probably comes as no surprise that a lot of effort goes into providing a quality outdoor play area. Most traditional preschools have an outdoor play area but are not what a nature-based educator would define as "quality."

Traditionally, preschool play areas include elaborate and very expensive climbing structures where there are few movable toys or materials to manipulate. At an NBP, you will not see permanent manufactured climbing structures. Instead, you will see a largely natural space with few fixed elements and a wide variety of loose parts. These elements and loose parts are both man-made, such as a small playhouse, buckets, and shovels, and natural, such as hollow logs for crawling through, sticks, and leaves.

The natural play area provides a larger array of play opportunities than the traditional climbing structure. The emphasis shifts to a balance between physical activity—the typical focus of traditional equipment—and imaginative play. Both types of play areas support gross motor development, but natural play areas offer movable, ever-changing physical problems for children to solve while engaging them cognitively, socially, and emotionally.

In a large outdoor space with a variety of materials available, you will likely see fewer conflicts among children. While researchers are still exploring the reasons for this phenomenon, we can surmise that it happens because there is more physical space, less competition over resources, and less overall sensory input than in other outdoor play areas. This reduction in conflicts allows for deeper, more meaningful teacher-child and child-child interactions—which ultimately means richer learning.

There are many considerations when designing or enhancing an outdoor play area to be more aligned with a nature-based approach. The elements should support children's learning in a meaningful way, adhere to licensing regulations, and allow for appropriate risk in children's play. Although this section of the chapter will address each of these aspects of a high-quality natural play area, it will not discuss details of design, such as which elements or plants to include. If you choose to begin enhancing your outdoor play area, I encourage you to explore the many wonderful resources available that provide this level of detail. (See Appendix B.) You will find that it's not necessary to invest large amounts of money. Rather, through the intentional selection of quality elements, you can create an outdoor play area that supports the pedagogy of a nature-based program.

Broadly speaking, the outdoor play area should have a natural feel rather than traditional playground equipment, should be representative of the local place, and should be as rich with learning and teaching opportunities as a typical indoor space. The outdoor space should be an extension of the classroom that is just as critical to teaching and learning as the indoor space. If it does these things, then it is no longer a play space that is located outdoors; it is a natural play area. Again, a well-designed natural play area will inherently result in fewer conflicts among children, more engaged play, and deeper learning.

State Regulations and Licensure

Inevitably, when I talk with teachers about moving the outdoor play area toward a more nature-based approach, there are questions about licensing regulations. While I would love to give a broad blanket statement about what is and is not allowed in a natural play area, that is impossible. Each state and province is different. I can say, however, that whatever you do should absolutely adhere to your area's regulations. Typically states require preschools to adhere to the national playground inspection standards. While this is appropriate for built structures, the standards do not account for things like logs and stumps. Exciting for the field of NbECE is that some states, such as Michigan, now address this challenge by including definitions and rules for natural play areas in their regulations.

Check your state's regulations, and talk with your licensing inspector as you're planning changes to your natural play area. Remember that licensing regulators want children to have quality learning opportunities that are safe. Start from this place of common ground as you discuss the possibilities.

Design Principles

There are a few essential elements for creating an effective natural play area. The outdoor play area is an extension of the indoor classroom and a classroom in and of itself. As such, it should provide opportunities for creative expression, building with blocks and other materials, literacy, science, math, music, and so on. In addition, the natural play area should provide opportunities for gross motor play. There are a few design features to consider in creating a truly effective natural play area.

- Safety

- Appropriate sizing

- Proximity to other learning areas

- Variety of spaces

- Variety of natural features

- Variety of materials

- Opportunities for engagement with all developmental domains

- Opportunities for risky play

The next several sections discuss these principles.

Safety

First and foremost, any natural play area should be safe. This does not mean that there are no opportunities for risky play; it does mean that hazards have been removed. Hazards are things that are likely to harm children and that children cannot control or are not expecting to be there. These include, for example, dead branches hanging overhead, poison ivy, and wasp nests. They also include human-related hazards such as broken glass and pet feces. Additionally, consider traffic and fumes from parking lots when determining where to locate the play area. I'm a fan of fencing the natural play area. This sometimes surprises people, but my reasoning is quite simple: having a fence allows teachers to be a bit more engaged in children's play. This is not to say that teachers are suddenly "off duty" and may stop being on alert to the whole class. It is simply to say that a fence buys a few more seconds of teacher-child interactions and conversation.

Remember, children have opportunities for open, unfenced experiences in the beyond. The fenced play area provides peace of mind by establishing a clear boundary. Ideally, whatever fence you choose will have a natural look and not interfere with the general appearance of a natural space. Consider, for example, a split-rail fence with field fencing or simple field fencing alone.

While hazards are generally things children cannot control and that we remove for them, this does not mean we leave children out of the conversation. It's essential that we engage them in analysis of risk. Talk with children, for example, about why an overhanging branch is potentially dangerous. Help children learn to identify—and avoid—poison ivy and other potentially harmful local plants. Teach them what to do if they see an unexpected hazard, such as broken glass. In some parts of the world, natural hazards such as venomous snakes and spiders are a fact of life. While it is possible to mitigate these hazards, such as by installing special fencing along the base of the play-area fence to prevent some snakes from entering, it is also important for adults and children to be engaged. Teach children, for example, what poison oak looks like, how to avoid it, and what to do if they come into contact with it.

Hazards to Remove from the Natural Play Area

While each region has different hazards to be aware of, here are a few of the most common hazards that should be identified and removed from play areas.

Plant and Fungi Hazards

- Dead overhanging branches
- Skin-irritating plants (such as poison ivy, poison oak, poison sumac, and hogweed)
- Poisonous plants and mushrooms (such as pokeweed and poison hemlock)

Animal Hazards

- Stinging insects (such as hornets and wasps)
- Venomous snakes
- Venomous spiders
- Other venomous animals (such as scorpions)

Human-Created Hazards

- Broken glass
- Used needles or condoms
- Pet feces

Appropriate Sizing

The play area should be large enough to provide ample space for each child who might be playing there. This means that if a play area will occasionally house multiple classes at once, the space needs to be large enough for those times.

Children need room to fully engage in gross motor movement. They need to be able to pick up speed, run, skip, and leap. Having ample space supports these learning opportunities. If you find your natural play area is too small, consider simply extending the current boundaries. If that is not possible or practical, perhaps there is a space away from the building that could be fenced. The class could then walk to that space for the outdoor-play portion of the day. The downside of this option is the distance from the indoor space, which brings me to the third design feature.

Proximity to Other Learning Areas

In a perfect world, the indoor classroom would open directly to the outdoor play area. Unfortunately, for most programs this is not feasible. Many programs, however, do have relatively easy access between the indoor and outdoor space. The strength of this design is that it supports blurring indoor and outdoor learning. If a child remembers a toy indoors that she'd like to integrate into outdoor play, she can easily retrieve that toy (with adult supervision, of course). Easy access to the indoors allows for sharing play materials and helps in meeting logistical needs, such as getting extra clothing when a child gets too wet. Locating the outdoor play space near the indoor space allows you to provide a wider variety of play materials without having to stock duplicates.

Thus far, I've focused on the interaction between the indoor and outdoor areas. Ideally, the natural play area would open directly to the beyond space as well. Many preschools can only enter or leave the outdoor play area by going through the building. The simple addition of a gate to the outdoor play area can allow quicker access to the beyond space. This not only eases the logistical transition by not having to traipse through the building, but it also makes for a smoother psychological transition between outside and beyond.

Variety of Spaces

While each natural play area should reflect the geographic and sociocultural place where it is located, all outdoor play areas should include a variety of spaces. These universal spaces not only support children's physical development but also support children's cognitive and social-emotional development through problem solving, creative thinking, and social interaction.

- Sunny and shady areas

- Muddy and dry areas

- Rough areas, such as piles of rocks and pebbles or dirt areas for digging

- Soft areas, such as sand boxes or grassy spaces

- Seating areas

- Nook-like spaces

- Large-group gathering spaces

- Hard surfaces for riding wheeled toys (if your program has them)

- Horizontal surfaces for fine-motor explorations

- Open areas for gross-motor play

Provide soft seating areas that support engaging with an adult or another child or two. Create nook-like spaces where children feel like they are able to hide from the group. (Keep in mind this is a feeling of being separate, not actual separation.) Provide a space where a large group can meet and engage in whole-group discussions and activities, such as a circle of whole logs, straw bales, or stumps buried approximately a third of their height in the ground. The natural play area should also include hard surfaces such as hard-packed dirt or even finely crushed gravel where children can play with wheeled toys. For fine motor development, include horizontal surfaces, such as child-sized picnic tables, the top of a smooth tree stump, or benches, where children can sit or stand to write or explore small natural items. Provide large spaces that allow for running and vestibular movement such as swinging, skipping, riding wheeled toys, and so forth.

Popular features in natural play areas include a sand box, mud kitchen, stump circle, logs for balancing, wooden boats, miniature log cabin, music station, and stage for dramatic play performances. In the end, the mix of spaces will vary from program to program, but the key is to have a variety of spaces so that a variety of developmental domains are supported through children's play.

Variety of Natural Features

Include a mix of natural features. As much as possible, the play area should have a general look and feel of a true natural space rather than a manicured park. This means including local varieties of vegetation, such as trees, shrubs, grasses, and flowers. Provide rocks, logs, different soil types, and water to support a variety of play as well. If possible, offer changes in topography, such as a small hill and a flat area. A small hill might be used for rolling down in the fall and sledding in winter when there is snow on the ground.

There are a few considerations to keep in mind when planning for a variety of natural features. First, choose plants with care and an awareness of both the immediate and long-term implications. Opt for plants that are safe for children to handle, provide a variety of textures, and grow to different heights. Consider what the plant will produce that will be interesting for play or that may be problematic in some way. For example, an oak tree will produce acorns, which will be great loose parts for play. A female ginkgo tree, on the other hand, will emit a rotten stench when it drops fruit and leaves in the fall. Include a designated garden area, as well. This garden area could be planted, maintained, and harvested by children throughout the growing season.

Second, consider how you will safely provide the children with access to water. Many states have specific rules on the inclusion of water elements in play areas, so be sure to consult your local regulations. Ideally, children will have free access to water like any other material, but of course this means the water depth is a safety concern. For this reason, I am a big fan of rain barrels that store water, allow children free access, and provide a connection both to the natural world (Has it rained recently?) and children's behavior (Did someone leave the spigot on?). In addition to access, keep your climate in mind. Will a water feature evaporate in your dry climate? Will standing water become a breeding ground for mosquitoes? Will the barrel fill up with fallen leaves? What can be done to mitigate these issues? Screens to cover rain barrels, for example, can be purchased to prevent the water from filling with debris.

Third, as much as possible, create features that resemble the natural world. Remember this outside space is in the middle of the continuum between highly structured indoor space and very unstructured beyond space. So there will be some structure, but it should be much less rigid than the indoor space.

Variety of Materials

A quality natural play area has a variety of materials available for children to access and use in their play. These materials should include both natural and human-made items and be primarily made up of loose parts. *Loose parts*, a term coined by landscape architect Simon Nicholson, refers to any material that can be manipulated and does not serve just one purpose. Buckets, shovels, ropes, spoons, and cups, for example, are all man-made loose parts. Sand, soil, sticks, leaves, and rocks are natural loose parts. The combination of both human-made and natural

---

Loose Parts

Human-made

- Buckets in a variety of sizes
- Shovels
- Rakes
- Ropes
- PVC pipes, both whole and cut in half lengthwise (don't forget connectors and elbows)
- Spoons
- Cups
- Bowls
- Muffin tins
- Bundt pans
- Whisks
- Strainers
- Buttons
- Nuts and bolts
- Crates

Natural

- Sand
- Soil
- Sticks
- Logs (sized so children can move them easily)
- Leaves
- Stumps
- Seashells
- Tree cookies (a cross-section of a log that is just a few inches thick)
- Rocks in a variety of sizes
- Acorns
- Seed pods
- Samaras, the official name for maple seeds (or "helicopters," as children call them)
- Pinecones

materials supports both rich, imaginative play and nature investigation. The natural materials will provide homes for a variety of animal and plant life (a good thing!), and the human-made materials, such as magnifying glasses, will support the investigation of those organisms.

When developing the natural play area, don't forget to add materials typically found inside the classroom, such as writing and art supplies, books, and musical instruments. A helpful question to ensure a variety of materials in the natural play area is, "Are all of the areas found in the indoor classroom represented outside as well?" The answer to this question is hopefully an emphatic yes! To be clear, this does not mean the materials must be the same, but the basic activity should be the same in both spaces. The library area inside, for example, may have a variety of front-facing bookshelves with soft seating for reading. Outside, there may be a small bin of books that children can choose from. So while the display and number of books may vary, in both spaces children can access and read books of their choice. (We discuss more ways to incorporate literacy outdoors in the next section.) Your indoor art materials might include markers, crayons, and a variety of paper. You can make these items available outdoors as well, but the outdoors might also include a transient art area where children can make sculptures and artwork using natural loose parts.

Of course, for all children to engage in this rich play, you must provide a plentiful amount of materials so there is not undue competition. Yes, some competition for materials provides an opportunity to teach negotiation and conflict-resolution skills, but those moments should not be commonplace. Thinking about plentiful materials may have you wondering, "Where do I put all this stuff?" Outdoor storage is very helpful. Lockable sheds, benches that serve as both seating and storage, and plastic tubs will help you organize and store your materials. For those who lack sufficient outdoor storage, consider using wheeled suitcases for larger loose parts and a heavy-duty briefcase for consumable supplies. These cases can be taken inside at the end of the day for overnight storage.

While it may be logistically challenging to provide these materials daily, providing variety is important. Variety will allow children's imaginations to come alive in their play.

Opportunities for Engagement with All Developmental Domains

A necessary element in quality natural play-area design is the integration of all developmental domains, including all disciplines within the cognitive domain. In NBPs, the outdoor play area is truly an extension of the indoor space, not simply an area for motor development. By providing a variety of spaces, natural features, and materials, the outdoor play area supports child-child and adult-child interactions and thus supports social-emotional development. The outdoor play area also supports cognitive development and exploration in literacy, science, technology, engineering, math, and art. Here are some ways to support each area of development in the natural play area.

Social-Emotional Development

Like the indoor classroom, natural play areas provide many opportunities for child-child and adult-child interactions. These encounters help children develop their understanding of social norms and appropriate peer-to-peer interactions as they build skills such as cooperation, problem solving with peers, and conflict resolution. Natural play areas also support more individual, intrinsic social-emotional development, such as building self-regulation. While risky play is typically thought of as a physical-development activity, it also supports social-emotional development, and natural play areas provide an excellent space for it. Risky play helps children build confidence, persistence, and experiences with reading their own emotions and doing "gut checks" before taking risks. I discuss risky play in more detail later in this chapter.

Language and Literacy

Many nature-based programs have a bin of books kept in the outdoor storage area. Others have a covered library storage area, much like the Little Free Libraries popular in communities across the United States. Still others have converted storybooks to "all-season" books by laminating the pages. Support opportunities for writing by providing small, portable dry-erase boards and markers; chalkboard paint on the tops of smoothed off stumps; or a vertical easel with paints or markers. Language and literacy supports do not have to be limited to consumable or transient materials. Consider providing more permanent features such as wooden letters that children can move to spell words along a fence. Plant an alphabet garden, for example, where each plant represents or is in the shape of a letter.

Science, Technology, Engineering, and Math

When designing a natural play area, consider science, technology, engineering, and math (STEM) learning opportunities as well. Magnifying glasses, a variety of containers, and "bug boxes" support exploration of animal life within the play area. Provide materials and spaces for collecting, sorting, and classifying, which are important skills in science and math development. Egg cartons or muffin tins are great tools for these

activities. Include elements that support weighing and measurement such as rain gauges, thermometers, and balances. These items are not only examples of technology in use, but they also support meaningful engagement with science and math. Additionally, large loose parts such as logs, boards, PVC pipes, ropes, and pulleys provide the materials for engineering explorations. Children might, for example, decide to build a fort or a system to haul materials across the play area.

Art Explorations

Of course, when supporting different cognitive domains, don't forget about opportunities for artistic expression. These can include easels, music stations, dancing scarves, puppets, a stage, and props for performances, as well as consumable artistic supplies such as markers, crayons, and paint. Keep in mind that, with the larger space outdoors, art projects can be done on a grander scale. Why not paint, for example, a giant refrigerator box or splatter paint on a bedsheet hanging on the fence?

Whatever fun activities lie ahead for your play with the children, I hope you'll keep in mind that the outdoor play area should not only support physical development. Just as the indoor space supports social-emotional and cognitive development, so should the outdoor play area—and in intentional, meaningful ways.

Opportunities for Risky Play

One unique and core component of NBPs is the opportunity for children to engage in risky play. Many people recoil a bit when they hear this—you *encourage* risky play? Yes, NBPs encourage appropriate, beneficial risky play. This does not mean encouraging dangerous play; it means encouraging

play that requires children to engage cognitively in their physical activity. Risky play allows children to connect with the feeling in their gut that tells them whether or not to do something. They can attempt a task multiple times and then have the feeling of success when they finally accomplish it. Risky play also helps children build creative problem-solving skills and engage in self-discovery. Many other authors, such as Tim Gill and Ellen Sandseter, have written about the power of risky play, and I encourage you to read their work.

What is lost if children never experience the learning moments that risky play provides? In her article "Characteristics of Risky Play," Ellen Sandseter defines *risky play* as "thrilling and exciting forms of play that involve a risk of physical injury." Inherent in risky play is the chance a child will get hurt. What we often do not consider is the risk of injury that we cause by not allowing risky play. This injury is not a physical wound but an emotional one. We are putting children at emotional risk when we prevent them from experiencing opportunities to challenge themselves. Physical injuries are relatively easy to recover from—our bodies heal. But how does a child recover from never learning how to persist with a challenging problem or never learning to read that feeling in her gut that tells her whether to do something? Those are much harder injuries to overcome.

Risks are things that could cause injury but also provide a physical, cognitive, or social-emotional reward. (In contrast, recall that *hazards* are those things that are both likely to harm children *and* unexpected or out of the children's control.) In risky play, children have the power to prevent injury through their own decision making and behaviors. Ellen Sandseter, a researcher from Norway, has identified six types of risky play: great heights, high speed, dangerous tools, dangerous elements, rough-and-tumble play, and disappearing or getting lost. Since our topic in this chapter is play-area design, we focus on providing and supporting different types of risky-play opportunities.

Great Heights

This type of risky play involves activities such as climbing, standing on, or jumping from raised surfaces and hanging or swinging up high. All of these actions involve the risk of falling, and this risk should be part of any benefit-risk analysis that you and the children conduct before engaging in these activities.

Good climbing trees are ideal spaces for this type of play, but they take time to establish in a play area. In the meantime, you can begin to provide opportunities for great-heights play by providing stumps or large rocks in the play area. Children can stand up on or jump off of these objects.

High Speed

Young children thrill at going fast, and this category of risky play captures that idea. With high speed comes the risk of colliding with someone or something. When conducting benefit-risk analyses with children, discuss how to avoid crashes during this type of play.

High-speed play might include swinging, riding tricycles or scooters, or running really fast. Keep these activities in mind as you develop the play area and the rules for play within that area.

Dangerous Tools

With guidance from adults, using dangerous tools can be a powerful experience in learning responsibility and safety—not to mention in developing skills related to the use of specific tools. Tools such as knives, saws, axes, and ropes all pose a risk of injury, yet they help children build and create things. While some NBPs have these tools available to children at all times, most provide dangerous tools occasionally at the beginning of the year and scaffold children's skill development with the tools as they slowly build up to daily tool use. For example, to support children in learning to whittle wood with knives, many programs begin by having children learn to safely use potato peelers. Once children have demonstrated competency with the program's safety protocols and the peelers, they can move on to knives. Most nature-based programs choose to stick with tools such as hammers, screwdrivers, and saws and only use these tools on occasion—not on a daily basis.

Dangerous Elements

Fire pits, deep water, and cliffs are all examples of dangerous elements. While dangerous elements all pose a risk of injury, most of this kind of risk will be rare in an NBP. However, you might choose to have a fire with the children on occasion. Roasting marshmallows while sitting around a fire is a great way to build community while experiencing this type of risky play.

Rough-and-Tumble Play

Rough-and-tumble play includes activities such as wrestling or using sticks as swords. Though these types of activities carry a risk of injury, rough-and-tumble play has fortunately been getting more positive attention in early childhood lately. All children, boys and girls, need the opportunity for this kind of play.

To move toward allowing more rough-and-tumble play outdoors, perhaps designate part of the natural play area for "sword" fighting, wrestling, and similar activities. As with all kinds of play, clear expectations need to be established for how children will keep themselves and each other safe.

Disappearing or Getting Lost

From your own childhood, you may remember the thrill of feeling as though you could be away from adult supervision. Children need that feeling. While we do not want to truly provide opportunities for them to get lost, we can provide them with the sensation of being alone. Hidden, cozy spots in the play area where two or three children can meet can provide this feeling. See-through fabric draped over a branch, for example, provides children with the feeling of being hidden while allowing for adult supervision.

Moving toward a Natural Play Area

After reading the suggestions for natural play-area design, you may find yourself overwhelmed and thinking, "How can we possibly do this?" Remember, you're moving toward a nature-based approach. That does not mean the natural play area must be converted from built structures to natural elements overnight.

My recommendation is to start small and see how things go. What are the children drawn to? What is inspiring for the teachers? In most cases, starting small will mean integrating natural and human-made loose parts, then adding some natural features later. Eventually you might be able to convince the powers that be (whether that's you or a supervisor) to eliminate the playground structures. As you begin to make small changes in the physical environment, you'll see positive differences in children's play and teacher-child interactions. These differences may take time, so be patient with both the children and your colleagues. Don't assume that because on day one the children didn't play with the new pile of soil that the change was a failure—be patient!

Frequently Asked Questions

1. **How do I find out what my local regulations are for play areas?** Your state's licensing regulations will outline rules for outdoor play areas. If you're unsure about something, talk to your licensing agent for specific guidance. Fortunately, some states are now developing specific definitions for natural play areas and regulations tailored to this type of outdoor play space. Again, consult your licensing agent to learn if your state has these rules and, if so, where to find them.

2. **Children love traditional climbing structures, and we already have one in our outdoor play area. Is it okay to leave it and simply add natural play features around it?** Most likely your state regulations will allow this, but you'll want to verify it. Regulations often stipulate that traditional playground equipment and natural play areas must be in distinct zones rather than together. In other words, the traditional playground equipment would be in an area separate from natural elements, such as a stump circle.

3. **Where do I find natural materials like logs?** Private tree-service companies, city forestry departments, and so on are often happy to keep an eye out for logs. They may also be willing to cut stumps for a stump circle or tree cookies (thin slices of log) for loose-parts play. Local landscaping or sand and gravel companies may be willing to help with materials such as sand and soil. Don't forget that your students' families may also be a great resource for natural materials.

4. **What common mistakes should I avoid when creating a natural play area?** The biggest mistake I see programs make is rushing in to spend lots of money and make everything perfect from day one. Take your time, start small, invest in a big item or two at a time, and then let the children guide the continued development of the area through their needs and interests. Remember, a natural play area is a constantly evolving space. The second-biggest mistake is forgetting that loose parts are a vital component of a natural play area. Simply having a few structures will not make for rich play—there must be loose parts as well. Another common mistake I see in natural play areas is a lack of teacher-child interactions. Time in the natural play area is not recess but an extension of classroom learning. As such, there should numerous ongoing teacher-child and child-child interactions in this space.

Reflections on Practice

1. What land, facilities, and landscaping does my school's play area already have?

2. Does the play area have the general feel of being a natural space versus a human-built environment?

3. What land, facilities, and landscaping do we need to add or modify to make a true natural play area?

4. Are there any regulations in my location that the natural play area must adhere to?

5. What land, facilities, and landscaping do we need to add or modify to meet regulations?

6. Are there hazards that need to be removed to make the space safe?

7. How close is the outdoor space to the indoor and beyond spaces? How could I increase the access to and movement among these spaces?

8. What types of spaces does the play area provide? What are the natural features in the space?

9. How many loose parts are included in the natural play area? Is there a wide variety of nature-made and human-made loose parts?

10. What are the opportunities available for the various developmental domains?

11. What opportunities for risky play are available in the outdoor play area?

Chapter 7:
THE CLASSROOM BEYOND

In addition to time in the outdoor play area, children in an NBP have daily experiences with natural spaces beyond the boundaries of a fenced play area. These experiences connect children to the wilder, more authentic natural world around them. In the beyond, the pace slows, the noise of the human-built world is reduced, and the wonders of the natural world are amplified.

While the destination may vary from day to day, the children visit these same ecosystems over the course of a year. As a result, children notice seasonal changes over time. In early fall, for example, children might visit a pond and notice colorful leaves floating on the surface. A month or so later, a child might point out the floating ice "pancakes" beginning to form. Midwinter, they might realize the ice is thick enough to walk on, and in spring the same pond is host to singing red-wing blackbirds and thousands of freshly hatched tadpoles.

The teaching and learning that occurs in these spaces also varies from day to day. Some days, the teachers may direct a very specific activity, such as noticing and documenting the features of tadpoles. At other times, the children may choose the destination and what they will do along the way and once they've arrived. Generally, the beyond is for exploring, discovering, and experiencing something bigger than ourselves.

These regular experiences and seasonal connections help create a sense of place and belonging among children. This connection builds ownership, and if that ownership is nurtured, it will lead to individual agency and a willingness to act on behalf of that place. As David Sobel says in *Beyond Ecophobia: Reclaiming the Heart in Nature Education*, "What's important is that children have an opportunity to bond with the natural world, to learn to love it and feel comfortable in it, before being asked to heal its wounds. . . . Our problem is that we are trying to invoke knowledge, and responsibility, before we have allowed a loving relationship to flourish." Time in the beyond is foundational in developing children's bond with the natural world.

The beyond space is the most powerful of the three spaces, providing the most opportunities for children to have meaningful experiences learning *with* nature. Given that the beyond is the least human-structured of the three physical spaces, preparing the physical environment in this space is primarily focused on access to a variety of ecosystems, safety in those spaces, and loose parts to support exploration and discovery. Because nature does the work in providing the physical environment, this chapter focuses on considerations for an effective experience in the beyond.

Appropriate Beyond Space

Access to natural wild ecosystems is preferred for time in the beyond. Sometimes educators hear the term *wild* and assume I mean a pristine, expansive forest. While that would be wonderful, that is not necessary for a quality beyond space. At minimum, the beyond space should be large enough that children feel as though they are in another space separate from the human-built play area. This beyond space will feel secluded for the children, away from parking lots, roads, and pedestrian traffic. The beyond space should be a moderately healthy ecosystem without an overabundance of invasive species. The biodiversity in the beyond space will serve as another teacher, so an unhealthy ecosystem will limit children's learning opportunities. That being said, in most cases an experience in a less-than-perfect space is still better than no beyond experience at all. So don't write off the half-acre plot behind the school simply because it seems too small or lacks biodiversity.

An educationally valuable beyond space might be an empty lot neighboring the school, a neighborhood park, a local nature center, a nearby camp, or a state park. While not fully immersive in nature, human-built natural spaces such as an arboretum, farm, or

Potential Beyond Sites

Here are some possible areas to use as a "beyond" space. Of course, you should always talk to the owners to secure permission and any necessary permits before beginning to use an area.

- City parks
- County parks
- State or national parks
- Nature centers
- Private land
- Public schools (some schools have natural spaces separate from the manicured school grounds)
- Local, regional, or national land conservancies

zoo are also possibilities for beyond spaces. Remember, the goal of the beyond is to have experiences in natural wild spaces, but these experiences are also on a continuum. Use the wildest space available to you—whatever that may be.

Activities in the Beyond

The purpose of time in the beyond is to develop children's meaningful relationships with a particular place through experiences that build over time. Having these experiences requires teaching and learning that varies from day to day. These activities vary not only in learning *in*, *about*, and *with* nature but also in who is leading the activity. Some days teachers may provide materials and ideas for a specific activity; other times, the children may choose the destination and activities.

For example, a heavily teacher-led activity—one that I would describe as learning *in* nature—would be searching for missing letters scattered throughout the woods. With this activity, the teacher has a clear purpose, provides the materials, and offers little opportunity for child choice. It's an activity that could easily be conducted in any physical environment—even indoors. An activity that would be more aligned with learning *with* nature is taking nets, dippers, and buckets to explore a pond. In this case, the teachers provide materials and a general purpose, but there is a great deal of child choice and creativity within the activity. Depending on the level of teacher direction, this could be a combination of learning *about* and *with* nature. Moving even closer to a child-led activity might be visiting an area of a forest, giving the children no prompts or direction, and allowing them to explore in any way they choose.

While all three of these examples are appropriate for an NBP, the goal is to have a mix of learning *in*, *about*, and *with* nature, emphasizing child-led

activities over teacher-led ones. The beyond is primarily for exploring and discovering, for children and teachers experiencing the wilder natural world. As a result, activities in the beyond will likely be child-led, discovery-based activities—learning *with* nature.

Safety Considerations

The beyond space is the least structured of the three learning spaces in an NBP. It is also the space most likely to be changed by natural occurrences and the influence of outside people. The beyond is also the space least regulated by licensing and regulatory agencies. These factors mean there is even more pressure on educators to maintain safety—more so than in any other space we've discussed previously.

Before leaving the natural play area, educators must ensure that staff members have appropriate training for managing any potential safety issues that may arise on the trail. This includes proper training in outdoors skills and organizational safety protocols related to activities in the beyond. These site-specific protocols outline how you will identify and remove hazards from these areas. Protocols will also identify appropriate teacher-to-child ratios, procedures for keeping the group together, what to do if a child needs to use the bathroom, how to engage children in benefit-risk assessments, establishing boundaries in areas with no fences, and so much more. You may, for example, have a policy that there must always be a teacher at the front and the back of the group and that these teachers must be able to see each other at all times.

If done well, the written policies and procedures for experiencing the beyond not only describe appropriate procedures but also identify safety materials that should always accompany the group.

Choosing and Carrying Supplies

For most programs, needed materials are carried in a trail bag of some sort, such as a backpack. At minimum, this critical bag will include basic safety items such as a first-aid kit, a two-way radio or cell phone for contacting the preschool office, and children's emergency paperwork. This bag may also include spare gloves and hats, facial tissues, hand sanitizer, extra snacks, and so forth. Consider including comfort items, such as hand warmers for really cold days, extra hats and gloves, or an extra pair of socks. Of course, you may also include resources to enhance teaching, such as containers for collecting insects, a dry-erase board and marker for writing, and natural-history reference books.

Consider including items to support impromptu learning that may occur while out and about in the beyond. These teachable moments—the moments you were not planning for but that the natural world provides on a moment's notice—are what make time in the beyond so incredibly powerful. Items to support teachable moments might include magnifying glasses, a track identification book, a camera, and a plastic jar for collecting interesting organisms (that you will, of course, return to their natural habitats).

If you have a specific activity or destination in mind and need to carry more materials and gear, I have found that a sturdy wagon with all-terrain wheels is the most effective for hauling items into the beyond.

This allows for oversized items that might be difficult to carry or put in a backpack and gives the children the opportunity to share responsibility for getting the materials to the destination. The wagon can also serve as a nice visual marker for group management in terms of boundaries or a meeting spot.

What you put in the wagon depends on your destination and the expected activity you'll engage in. If you're going to a meadow, for example, it may be appropriate to bring items for insect collection, such as sweep nets, aerial nets, old white bedsheets (so that the children can see the insects against them), bug boxes, hand lenses, and identification books. If you're visiting a forest with no real activity goal in mind, you might bring spoons for digging, hand lenses, a storybook or two for children who would like to read, some writing materials, and maybe rope or string for those children who would like to build. I realize I've just provided a wide array of materials for taking into the beyond. There is no scripted answer for what to bring; pay attention to children's interests and

adapt your materials accordingly. The best way to do this, of course, is to ask children before leaving, "What should we take with us into the beyond?" When children are first experiencing the beyond, they may need support in generating ideas, but I assure you that once they've become familiar with the beyond, they will have a plan in mind and will be very willing to offer a list of materials to take along.

Increasing Your Time in the Beyond

Ideally, experiences in the beyond occur daily and access to the area is direct—meaning you open the gate of the natural play area and immediately enter the beyond space. For many programs, however, direct access is not possible. For some programs, a brief walk will get them there. For others, the walk may be a little longer. If walking to and from the beyond, such as a local park, takes away too much time from other activities, consider asking parents to either drop off or pick up their children at the park. This would result in children walking one way rather than round-trip.

For those programs just moving toward a nature-based approach and without walkable access to a natural area, going to the beyond may be a quarterly day-long field trip to a local nature center, park, or other natural area. Over time, if financial resources allow, these field trips can be increased in frequency to every month rather than quarterly. There are many kindergarten and first-grade classes who now visit the beyond for a full day once each week. This is a model that might be helpful for preschools looking to integrate more time in the beyond. These "forest Fridays," "meadow Mondays," or "wilderness Wednesdays" allow children to regularly immerse themselves in a natural space and allow programs to accommodate the reality of logistics. Moving along the continuum, excursions can be available every day if the program provides transportation on a daily basis to access a distant beyond space. This might start as a small group of children and then eventually become the entire class.

As you're planning how to move along the continuum to more frequent visits to a consistent beyond space, remember that the goal is to support children in building a relationship with a particular place over time. The more children can visit that place, the better. Ultimately, to integrate more time in the beyond space, identify the barriers, such as access, safety, and time, and slowly start making changes toward daily integration of experiences in the beyond.

Frequently Asked Questions

1. **How wild does a space have to be to "count" as the beyond?** Any space outside the natural play area where nature is primarily guiding the materials and experiences can "count" as the beyond. That being said, the wilder or more natural the space, the better. The wilder the space, the more likely it is that impromptu teachable moments will arise for children to learn *with* nature.

2. **My NBP is in an urban area with little or no access to nature, and we have limited school transportation. How can I get my students into the beyond?** While walking right out the gate of the natural play area into the beyond is ideal, it's not always a possibility. Is there a beyond space relatively close to your building where family members and guardians could drop off or pick up children? If not, perhaps start with a quarterly field trip to a local nature center or park. Over time, you can build up to more-frequent visits to your beyond space. I know of one program, for example, that is in a very urban area, but every day the teachers take about twelve children on a small bus to a local Scout camp, which serves as their beyond space. There are absolutely options for getting students to the beyond—it's a matter of how hard you're willing to work to overcome the logistics.

3. **During our beyond excursions, how do I help children who crave structure and predictability enjoy their experiences?** While there is unpredictability in terms of what you'll discover in the beyond, there is predictability in the overall experience. There should be routines to prepare for the trip, predictable places to find the teachers during these excursions, some type of activity each day, and then a return to the building. If students need additional structure, you could set up a "base camp" in the beyond: a place you always go to at the beginning of an excursion and that serves as your jumping-off point for further exploration. Some of the same supports that you would use indoors for children craving structure, such as photo schedules, can be helpful in the beyond as well.

4. **How do we handle bathroom needs during excursions to a beyond space that has no facilities?** Encouraging bathroom breaks before you venture into the beyond will help keep bathroom needs to a minimum. The reality, however, is that bathroom needs will occur. The good news is that "going" in the woods is a good life skill, so teach children how to do it properly. Peeing is fairly straightforward, and your policies will address location (off the trail, behind a designated tree, or wherever is appropriate for your program), privacy-related issues, and hand-washing procedures. Pooping in the woods is much more complicated, and most programs choose to return to the building when this need arises. After all, most excursions to the beyond are not covering great distances, so it does not take long to go back. I have, however, seen programs that choose to bring a camp-style potty chair, a pop-up tent for privacy, toilet paper, and water for handwashing into the beyond for these situations.

5. **What do we do if a child falls in a puddle and gets soaking wet?** Again, this is one of those realities in working with young children outdoors. The first concern is children's safety, and the second is their comfort. In terms of safety, the urgency to get into dry clothes will depend on the weather conditions. If temperatures are cold, you'll want to get the child into dry clothes immediately. If temperatures are warm, you may simply reduce the child's discomfort by emptying water out of her footwear and taking off her wet socks before you make your way back to the building so she can change clothes.

Reflections on Practice

1. What are possible beyond areas near my school?

2. What policies or regulations do I need to follow related to children leaving the school property?

3. What other factors might limit my ability to take children to the beyond—distance, transportation, anything else?

4. What are possible solutions for overcoming the barriers to visiting the beyond spaces I have identified?

PART III:
BRINGING IT ALL TOGETHER

In the first two sections of the book, we discussed philosophy, pedagogy, and preparing the physical environment. There are a few final details to be aware of when implementing an effective nature-based approach. This final section of the book addresses the details of day-to-day planning and implementation of the nature-based approach by teachers and of ensuring that families have the information and resources necessary to be effective partners in creating a positive experience for young children.

Chapter 8:
PLANNING THE DAY

Nature is at the curricular core of an NBP. That means seasonal happenings and children's experiences outdoors drive all planning and curriculum. Our role as adults, whether we are teachers or administrators, is to ensure that we are integrating those nature-based aspects while intentionally supporting children's learning. We will be most successful when we intentionally structure our day, provide appropriate and meaningful materials, and design developmentally appropriate activities for teacher-directed portions of the day. This chapter focuses on structuring the day in a way that values nature-based experiences, leveraging children's interests in our planning, and documenting the learning that occurs.

Typical Day at a Nature-Based Preschool

While the typical day at a NBP may vary slightly from program to program, there is a general structure that most programs follow. That said, there remains a great deal of flexibility for teachers and children to adjust the timing, location, and order of portions of the day and the activities within those portions. The exact timing will depend on the children's engagement, which is influenced by a host of factors, including age, time of the school year, day of the week, weather, proximity to a holiday break, and so on. The structure I provide here is for a three-hour half-day program. A full-day program would look very similar, with the addition of a lunch and rest time.

The location of many of the portions of the day can vary. Snack, for example, may occur indoors, outdoors, or in the beyond. Rest time can occur in any of the three areas as well. Yes, it will require some logistical planning to adhere to licensing requirements with mats, blankets, and so on, but it can be done!

There is also flexibility in the order that portions of the day occur. The only structural emphasis that I see as a "requirement" in an NBP is that the outdoor play and excursion to the beyond occur first. As with anything, what we do first gets more of our time, attention, and energy. If we value children's experiences outdoors, then we should make that our priority. Beyond that, you may decide, for example, that you want to offer a small-group activity prior to choice time rather than after. Adapt the order of experiences and activities to fit the children's interests, your priorities, and everyone's safety, but be consistent in the schedule once it is established.

In northern Minnesota, where winter brings deep cold, NBP programs adjust their schedules so outdoor play occurs when the sun has had a chance to warm things up a bit. This is a temporary change; in the fall and spring, when the weather is warmer, they have outdoor play first. They still emphasize the outdoor component and simply make a shift to keep the children safe and let them be fully engaged in outdoor learning.

Any changes you make to the schedule should, of course, be communicated to the children and, when possible, made in consultation *with* the children. The general structure of the day should be consistent enough from day to day that children know what is coming next and can communicate that with others. It should be common to hear children say things like, "After our hike, we get to have a snack!" or during outdoor play to hear a child say, "Teacher, where are we going on our hike today?" These are signs that there is a clear routine in the classroom.

Having said all of that, let's talk about each portion of the day.

Arrival and Sign-In

As with any preschool classroom, there are many transitions that occur throughout the day at an NBP. Arrival is an opportunity to set children up for success for the day and connect learning across the physical bounds. Most licensing agencies require parents to sign their children in. If we want to support children's individual identity development and their sense of agency in their world, why not have them sign themselves in as well?

Leverage arrival and sign-in to support meaningful parent-child interactions and child learning. Provide a dry-erase board or some other easily changeable, large visual prompt that includes the date and a brief overview of the day (as much as it's known at the start of class). This informs parents of the day's events and prompts parent-child interaction. To facilitate children's sign-in, provide a question of the day and a place for the children to write their responses. For example, ask children to predict how many insects they'll find on the hike to the meadow and provide space for them to add their names to a graph. Or ask children where they'd like to go on the hike today, and then tally the votes at the group meeting

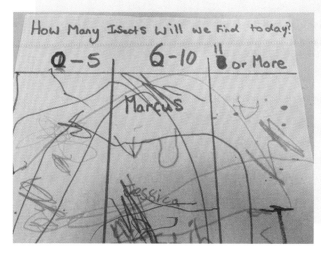

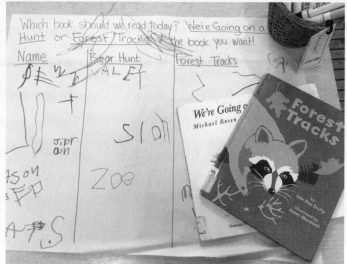

before heading out on the hike. These sign-in activities incorporate literacy by letting children practice writing their names; prediction, which is an important skill in science learning; and data graphing, which is both a science skill and a math skill, in meaningful ways.

Outdoor Play (45–60 Minutes)

When sign-in is completed, children can join their teachers, who are waiting, ready to play, in the natural play area. Though there are likely many more, I see four primary reasons for starting the school day outdoors rather than in the classroom.

First, time outdoors is the most valuable part of the day. Whatever we do first in our day receives the greatest amount of time and attention. In contrast, whatever we do at the end of the day will likely be rushed and receive less time than we'd planned. Second, we start with outdoor play because children are already dressed in their outdoor gear when they arrive at school. This results in one less transition in the day! The third reason to start outdoors is that latecomers will not disrupt the class flow but can simply join in play. Fourth, children can start the day on their own schedule and pace without an adult dictating the agenda. Many adults like to have a moment in the morning to drink a cup of coffee or tea and gather their thoughts before having someone else demand something of them. Children deserve that same courtesy. Having outdoor play first allows for that. I have seen some children who arrive, sign in, and then stand in the middle of the outdoor play area observing the different groups of children before committing to their play. On the other hand, I've seen children who arrive, sign in, and rush to their preferred play space. Every child is different, but having a choice first thing in the morning is important for all of them.

Group Meeting (5–15 Minutes)

The group meeting welcomes everyone to class for the day and prepares them for the excursion to the beyond. It's important to build a classroom community by welcoming the children, welcoming any guests, and acknowledging anyone who may be absent. Once this has been done, the class can move on to preparing for the excursion to the beyond.

The exact group activity will vary from day to day. The class might vote on their destination, for example, or read a story related to the adventure they're going to have. The group meeting will typically also include discussion about materials needed for their time in the beyond and any safety considerations. And the transition from the group meeting to leaving for a hike into the beyond will often include a final call for a bathroom break.

Excursion to the Beyond (45–60 Minutes)

Experiences in the beyond are intended to connect children to the wilder, authentic, natural world around them. These regular experiences help children build connections across seasons while being part of something greater than themselves, creating a sense of place and belonging among the children. Of course, providing experiences that build over time requires teaching and learning that varies from day to day. These activities vary not only in learning *in*, *about*, and *with* nature but also in who is leading the activity. Generally speaking, however, the beyond is for exploring and discovering natural world. As a result, most activities in the beyond will emphasize learning *with* nature—that is, child-led, discovery-based activities.

Transition to the Indoor Classroom

Most of the year at an NBP, the transition from outdoors to indoors occurs after the hike to the beyond, but again, the exact timing of this transition can vary. No matter when it occurs, I must point out a reality of this transition. Dirt happens. In fact, more dirt happens when more fun and learning happen. Just remember that children and clothing are washable. That being said, it's helpful to have a space outside the classroom where wet and muddy clothing can be removed. Then children can change into clean, dry clothing. Most NBPs also ask children to bring a separate pair of shoes for the indoor space. This helps minimize the mud, snow, sand, and so forth that make their way to the indoor classroom. It seems like a small point, but having a spot outside where children can change out of muddy gear will keep teachers, children, and administrators—and, more importantly, custodians—much happier!

Snack (15 Minutes)

Family-style snack may be held indoors, outdoors, or in the beyond. Children and teachers can use this time to talk about the shared experience they have had that day, so it is preferred that teachers do not read a book or try to conduct another lesson during snack. Discussions can range from, "Can you believe how close we were to those turkeys today? That one was really loud when it gobbled," to "Wow, wasn't it cold out today? It feels really warm inside now." Rich conversations about shared experiences support children in feeling a bond to the community and to the local environment.

Additional Free Play or Choice Time (30–60 Minutes)

The location of this choice time for play will vary depending on the weather. On really special days, children can play in the beyond. Typically, they can choose to play in the natural outdoor area or indoors. No matter the location, children in NBPs have the opportunity for the same free play typically found in quality indoor preschool spaces: blocks, art, literacy, science exploration, math manipulatives, music, and so on.

Small Groups (10–15 Minutes)

In a small-group activity, children complete a task or follow directions suggested by the teacher, using open-ended materials. While this is a teacher-directed part of the day, it still connects to children's interests and experiences in other parts of the day and allows for children to play and be creative. Children, for example, might be prompted to build an insect using natural loose parts, such as sticks, pinecones, or acorns. If they build an insect with twelve legs, that's okay, because the point is not to get to the "right" answer; the point is to be creative. Small group is an opportunity for directed time for teacher-child and child-child interactions that can highlight specific developmental domains. For example, if one child makes a twelve-legged insect and another child makes a six-legged insect, the teacher and children can engage in comparing numbers, sizes, and how fast one insect might walk compared to the other. As much as possible, small-group activities should connect to experiences children have had outdoors and the interests they have expressed in those spaces. This is another opportunity to connect the learning that happens in the indoors, outdoors, and beyond.

Final Group Meeting and Goodbye

The final group meeting is an opportunity to reflect on the day and wish each other well until the next time they gather. This might include a song or story related to the day, or children might share their favorite part of the day. Typically, it is a brief gathering, as most of the time has been spent having fun outdoors. As part of the farewell, some programs have the children sing a goodbye song—complete with local nature in the lyrics.

Teacher Planning

While planning time for teachers is not part of the children's day, it is important to include in the overall schedule. Ideally, the teaching team gathers at the end of each day to reflect on what learning occurred and how that learning could be extended or built on the next day. What were the children asking questions about? What seemed to draw their interest? The answers to these questions can guide teachers in determining what additional materials to provide during child-led choice times and what teacher-directed activities would be most appropriate for the next day's session.

NBP Example: Schlitz Audubon Nature Center Preschool

Location: Milwaukee, Wisconsin

Schlitz Audubon Nature Center Preschool is located on 185 acres on the shore of Lake Michigan and provides space for preschoolers to make discoveries in a variety of ecosystems. The three-to-five-year-old students attend half-day class sessions that are two hours and forty-five minutes long. Families choose two, three, or four days per week, each with two teachers and a maximum of sixteen children.

In partnership with BrainInsights, the Schlitz Audubon Center has created a set of activity cards that provide nature-based activities to help develop a child's brain, called *Naturally Developing Young Brains*. Each card has an activity on one side and a simply stated brain-development fact on the other.

Frequently Asked Questions

1. **My team doesn't have time to plan together daily. What is our next-best option?** Strive to plan together as often as possible. If daily planning is not an option, then perhaps you can meet every other day; if that is not possible, then try to meet weekly. If weekly planning is still problematic, then it may be time to evaluate and adjust your program and staffing structures to better allow for this important part of a nature-based curriculum.

2. **What do we do if the weather is too severe for outdoor time? For example, how can we handle a thunderstorm or strong winds that are hurling debris?** Before heading to the outdoor play area or into the beyond, always check the weather forecast. If the forecast is showing potentially hazardous weather, forgo the outdoor time for that day, or wait to venture out until after the storm has passed. (A good rule of thumb is to wait at least thirty minutes after hearing thunder before going outside.) If you get caught in an unexpected storm, find shelter as quickly as possible. Keep in mind that we are striving for safe, positive experiences outdoors—we are not trying to prove how tough we are.

3. **We don't have transportation away from school, so we visit the same beyond space every day. How do we keep it from becoming boring or repetitive to the children?** Visiting the same beyond space every day will allow the children to build an ongoing relationship with that place. Varying the loose parts available in the beyond can help keep this space from becoming boring. If the beyond space is large enough, most of those loose parts will come from the natural world. If the space is small or has minimal natural features, you may have to take more materials with you and perhaps even provide more activities focused on learning *in* or *about* nature.

Reflections on Practice

1. How does the current daily schedule match up with the suggested schedule in this chapter? What would we need to change to incorporate all the required blocks of time?

2. How much total time is currently spent outdoors each day?

3. Where does outdoor time occur in the current daily schedule?

4. What adjustments would need to be made to move outdoor time to first thing in the day (e.g., making breakfast available outdoors)?

5. What adjustments would need to be made to move snack, small-group, and choice time outdoors?

"We are visiting Japan. It is the rainy season here, so we are walking all over Kyoto in the rain. The rain does not bother my children. No such thing as bad weather. They find a snail. They find a stag beetle. They watch a heron fishing in the river. They see moss and hydrangea everywhere. They see how water runs in checkered patterns—and ask why. Nature preschool has formed the way my children see the world. For the rest of their lives, they will wonder. What greater gift is there than this?"

—Mika Y., Illinois, USA, *parent of two nature-based preschoolers*

Chapter 9:
SETTING FAMILIES UP FOR SUCCESS

NBP families consistently share their enthusiasm and love for the nature-based approach. While most of this enthusiasm stems from the foundational philosophy and pedagogy of nature-based education, family communication nurtures this enthusiasm. After all, any high-quality early childhood program recognizes that family involvement is key to fully supporting young children and must actively support family engagement as a result. Nature-based programs are no exception. For young children to thrive in an NBP, their families must be fully aware of and embrace the nature-based approach.

To ensure this engagement and enthusiasm, teachers and administrators must clearly communicate with families the philosophy and practices of the nature-based approach. Teachers and administrators must also ensure that children have the appropriate clothing for their time outdoors. Additionally, it's important for teachers and administrators to educate families on the need for the nature-based approach in children's lives and how families can build on the philosophies and practices at home.

Establishing Expectations

Communicating the philosophy and daily teaching practices of an NBP begins well before a family enrolls. Prior to enrollment, most families will make assumptions about the preschool and the nature-based approach based on the marketing and promotion of your program that they have seen. For this reason, any public marketing and promotion materials should be an accurate representation of a typical day at your program. Families should have a good idea of what your program involves and is all about.

Registration information and parent handbooks should also be clear in describing the overall philosophy of your program and a typical day. Include a mission and philosophy statement so families know the kind of community they'll be joining. Additionally, the typical day can be implicitly communicated by using images of children playing in all weather and in all settings and engaged in a variety of activities, including risky play. An image of a child jumping in a mud puddle on a gray late-winter day with mud and water splashing everywhere speaks volumes about the experiences children are likely to have in your program. Some might say an image like this turns some families away. That may be true, but it will also attract families who want to be part of your program. By providing an accurate image of your program, you're ensuring a mutual fit between the families and preschool.

Pre-Enrollment Open Houses

It's important to have open conversations with families about your philosophy, curriculum, and daily teaching practices. A great way to make space for these conversations is to host an open house where families can see the facilities—indoors, outdoors, and beyond—meet the teachers, and maybe even meet current families. Be clear with families that the open house is not an interview process but an opportunity for them to decide whether the program is a good fit for their family. Any open house should not be limited to adults; it should allow children to attend as well. Again, this comes back to living the philosophy that children are capable and should have agency in their individual lives.

Orientation

Once families have decided to enroll in your program, be clear about how they can be successful. This is true for a traditional preschool approach, of course, but it is particularly important in a nature-based setting, as it is different from what most people have experienced. Preschool programs can implement a variety of steps to help families make a smooth transition into a nature-based approach. A parent orientation during which families can learn about the ins and outs of your program is requisite. This is the one event where I suggest children do not attend so that parents can focus on the information being discussed. (I encourage you to offer child care if that is a barrier for families, but adults need time away from their children to concentrate.)

Parent orientation should include an overview of your teaching philosophy, a description of a typical day, a discussion about what emergent curriculum really means, explanations about how you support children's overall development and how you assess that development, descriptions of which activities are and are not allowed, a discussion of how you resolve conflict, and so forth. Talk with parents about clothing—what to provide and why (more on that in a moment). Parent orientation is also a chance for caregivers to meet the teachers who will be spending each day with their children. Do not underestimate parent orientation in the relationship-building process.

NBP Example: The Chippewa Nature Center's Nature Preschool
Location: Midland, Michigan

The Chippewa Nature Center's (CNC) Nature Preschool serves children ages three and four. Classes are three hours long and held two to four days per week. Most classes are mixed ages, but they do have a three-year-old-only and four-year-old-only class, with a teacher-to-child ratio of three to eighteen. Located on 1,300 acres, the program's main building houses two classes, and an additional classroom is located nearby on the nature center property. While the CNC's Nature Preschool is primarily tuition-based, some children in the program are funded through Michigan's Great Start Readiness Program which is designed to help at-risk four-year-old children receive a year of preschool education prior to kindergarten.

Each spring, the CNC hosts a multiday workshop called the Nature Preschool Institute, in which early childhood educators observe the program in action and learn ways to integrate the nature-based approach into their own practices.

Helping Families Transition to Your Program

Personally, I prefer that parent orientation be held a couple of weeks prior to the start of school. This leaves time for other transition activities such as home visits and another open house for currently enrolled families and their children. Both activities support children in building relationships with their teachers and ease the transition into attending school for the first time. Consider providing photos of the children's teachers and class pets. Some programs have been successful with starting half of the children on day one, the other half on day two, and then everyone on day three. None of these transition activities is unique to a nature-based approach, but they are effective parts of a quality early childhood program. In the end, your goal prior to enrollment and when families are first arriving is to make sure there is a mutual philosophical fit and that families have the information and resources they need to be successful.

> My advice to a future nature-based preschool parent? Buy some stain remover, proper weather gear, and lots of extra socks. Then, put your own hesitations aside and get to enjoying watching your child explore the natural learning environment around him. Take lots of pictures, talk every day about what your child saw or created, and be as involved as you can. Our current educational system is not built around the concepts of nature education, so this may be your child's only opportunity to learn in this unique way. Embrace it as fully as you can—your child certainly will."
>
> —Erin S., Michigan, USA, parent of a nature-based preschooler

Ensuring That Children Have Appropriate Clothing

In the NBP world, professionals will say children should wear appropriate clothing or even make statements such as, "There is no such thing as bad weather, just bad clothing." The fact of the matter is that most families, particularly with our societal disconnect from the natural world, do not know what *appropriate* or *good* clothing is. Our job is to teach them, so their children can thrive in preschool.

It's helpful to show families the layers of clothing children should wear for each season, reminding them that the in-between seasons are the hardest ones to dress for. Given the wide variety of climates within the United States and beyond, it's very difficult to provide you with specific clothing recommendations. The basic principle, however, of clothing selection is to help your body maintain its normal temperature at all times. This means keeping your body cool in hot temperatures and warm in cold temperatures. Teach parents the wisdom of adding or taking away layers of insulation, preventing contact with moisture, and protecting children from the wind.

Appropriate looks different in practice, depending on the climate. Families need to understand, for example, that materials such as cotton are terrible for wet seasons in more temperate climates, because the cotton will simply trap the moisture and make the children cold. A great example of this is those inexpensive stretchy cotton gloves. Those gloves might be appropriate for a dry fall day, but in temperate climates where cold temperatures and moisture are present for most of the year, those gloves simply trap moisture and make the child cold. Having clothing samples on hand for the families to actually touch is helpful for them to understand the differences in material. It's also helpful to provide recommendations on where they can find this appropriate clothing in your community or through online shopping sources. Even better is partnering with a clothing supplier to offer families a discount on items you have deemed as quality.

Weather Type	Possible Clothing List
Hot and dry	**Cool, minimal layer that protects from the sun** • Cotton T-shirt, shorts or pants, and socks • Linen long-sleeved overshirt • Sun hat
Warm or hot and humid	**Cool, minimal layer that wicks moisture away from the body and protects from the sun** • Synthetic moisture-wicking or cotton T-shirt • Nylon shorts or pants • Moisture-wicking socks, such as wool or wool-synthetic blends • Sun hat • Waterproof, breathable rain gear (jacket and pants or full-body rain suit) • Waterproof boots
Cold and wet	**Warm inner layers with waterproof outer layers** • Moisture-wicking base layers • Wool or synthetic (such as fleece) middle layers • Moisture-wicking socks, such as wool or wool-synthetic blends • Insulated, waterproof jacket and pants or breathable whole-body rain suit • Insulated, waterproof gloves and boots • Warm wool or synthetic hat
Cold and dry	**Warm layers** • Moisture-wicking base layers • Wool or synthetic (such as fleece) middle layers • Moisture-wicking socks, such as wool or wool-synthetic blends • Insulated, water-resistant jacket, pants, gloves, and boots • Warm wool or synthetic hat

There is no question that quality outdoor gear for children can be expensive. I often hear objections such as, "Our families are low-income and can't afford outdoor gear." First, stop and ask yourself, do you believe that experiences in nature are valuable to children's overall development? You're reading this book, so I'm assuming your answer is yes. Do you believe opportunities to write are important and thus you provide children with markers, pencils, crayons, and so on? Yes, of course you do. Outdoor gear is no different from other materials for successful learning. If quality gear is a financial burden or barrier for families, then the program should provide those materials just like any other learning resource in the preschool. This might mean buying class sets of rain suits, boots, hats, gloves, and so on. Many programs have had success securing grants for purchasing class sets of gear.

In contrast, providing clothing might mean that most families provide their own gear, but you can offer some families loaner gear for the school year. Even if all of your families are high-income and can easily provide children with quality gear, you will need extra clothing for any child who gets overzealous about a puddle. This means every program must have extra outdoor gear available, and a program with low-income families will just need a slightly larger supply of gear. I should mention here that it's helpful to have extra adult gear available too, so family members who volunteer can be prepared for the weather conditions.

Recommended Clothing Suppliers for Young Children

There are many different places to purchase outdoor gear for young children. Price points and quality vary, but these three companies are consistently good. My experience is they're also very supportive of NbECE.

- MyMayu, www.mymayu.com
- Oaki, https://oaki.com
- Polarin O. Pyret, www.polarnopyretusa.com

Ongoing Parent Education

Often programs think that once families have learned of your program and have committed to attending, the work is done, but that is far from the case. I understand how one might think the families "get" your philosophy and curriculum because they see it in action every day, but remember, these are parents, not early childhood professionals. Most parents do not have years of experience observing children as a means of understanding current development. Families are not with the children during the preschool hours, so they are unaware of the activities and learning that is occurring. Thus, it's our job to maintain ongoing communication and education with parents.

Of course, ongoing communication with families is a hallmark of any quality early childhood program, but in a nature-based setting the communication should also educate parents about the unique approach. This communication will include suggestions for building connections between school and home, particularly in support of engagement with the natural world. Our job is to help families understand why children need nature, what they learn through those experiences, and how families can extend the learning outside of the school day.

Communication with families can happen in many different ways. One approach is to provide families with weekly updates of activities, songs, books, and ideas that the children are engaged with. I find it useful to provide a brief—two- or three-sentence—summary of that day's plans at the adult and child sign-in station. This simple prompt opens the door for a conversation between the parent and child about the child's predictions for the day and provides a reminder for following up with the child at the end of the school day. Monthly newsletters are helpful and can include information about the benefits of time in nature. This might include articles you write or links to articles, book titles, blogs, or other resources where families can learn more about the nature-based approach. You can also provide information about local parks and nature centers where families might explore the natural world outside of the school day.

Another way to support the school-home connection is providing storybooks about nature along with suggestions of activities families could do at home related to the stories. A story about rocks, for example, might be accompanied by a prompt for searching for rocks in the backyard or neighborhood. You can give book-activity combinations to families to keep, but if budget is a limiting factor, these could also be something you loan to families for short periods of time.

Another way to involve families is to provide whole-family events outside of the school day. Often these events include food and a nature-based activity of some sort. Activity options include a weekend hike, an outdoor scavenger hunt, an outside guest to show live birds of prey, a concert with a musician who sings nature-based songs, a picnic at the local park, or even an overnight camping adventure. There are many options, and the limits are really time, staff availability, space, and the budget resources to make the events happen.

Finally, don't forget that family involvement during the class day is also a form of parent education. When families can see the program in action, they have a better understanding of what happens day in and day out. No matter how you choose to engage families, remember the goal is to encourage families to be part of children's learning outside of the school, ideally in a way that supports the nature-based approach.

Frequently Asked Questions

1. **A certain family seemed to be on board with our philosophy and practices when they enrolled their child in our program, but now they complain about their child getting dirty and other things that are normal in a NBP. How do we handle this?** I would have an open and honest conversation with this family. Are the complaints actually covering up a deeper issue that has nothing to do with the dirt? If not, what is it about getting dirty that is problematic? Perhaps there is a lot of stress at home and the added burden of dirt in the car and extra laundry is taking its toll. Ultimately, I would work to get to the root cause of the family's concerns and then address those accordingly.

In some cases, families think they have an understanding of the approach before enrollment, but reality is different from their expectations. Working together, you can problem-solve to determine the best path forward.

2. **A family wants to enroll a child with limited mobility in our program. Our natural play area and beyond areas have uneven ground and no pavement. How can we accommodate this child?**
I believe in having open conversations with the family—including the child. What is the range of the child's mobility? What changes could you make to the natural play area to allow this child to access all of the play area? This might, for example, be as simple as removing logs that border paths, enabling the child to leave a path without tripping or getting stuck. For trips to the beyond, would a wagon or other wheeled system allow the child to venture with the group to distances farther from the building? In the end, strive to include this child in ways that allow him to experience the natural world with minimal barriers and maximum independence.

Reflections on Practice

1. Do our marketing materials show that we go outdoors in all kinds of weather?

2. How do we discuss the value and role of nature during parent orientation?

3. What guidance do we give families on acquiring appropriate clothing?

4. What ongoing communication do we have with parents about the value and role of nature in our program?

5. Do we have enough extra clothing if families do not come prepared? If not, how can we secure these materials? Is there a local community foundation that might give us a grant? Would a local business be willing to donate some clothing?

Appendix A:
RESOURCES FOR NATURE-BASED ACTIVITIES

Below I have provided an annotated bibliography of nature-based activity books for inspiration when planning teacher-led activities. I provide these with the understanding that, after having read this book, you will use nature-based pedagogy to guide activity selection and help you articulate why you chose those activities. Remember, the goal is to create experiences for young children that emerge from their interests and ideas. There are three big pedagogical ideas to make this happen:

1. Daily responsive planning

2. Teacher-directed activities that are a mix of learning *in*, *about*, and *with* nature, but emphasize learning *with* nature

3. In-the-moment adjustments to whatever you had planned

With that in mind, here are some resources to investigate.

Banning, Wendy, and Ginny Sullivan. 2010. *Lens on Outdoor Learning*. St. Paul, MN: Redleaf.

> This book not only provides ideas for outdoor activities, but it also describes how those experiences relate to learning standards.

Chalfour, Ingrid, and Karen Worth. 2005. *Exploring Water with Young Children*. St. Paul, MN: Redleaf.

> This book provides ideas for helping children discover the properties and behavior of water.

Cornell, Joseph. 1989. *Sharing Nature with Children*. Nevada City, CA: Dawn Publications.

> This is a classic book in the environmental education world and provides a variety of sensory-based activities to conduct with children.

Cornell, Joseph. 2015. *Sharing Nature: Nature Awareness Activities for All Ages*. Nevada City, CA: Crystal Clarity.

> Another classic in the environmental education world, this book also provides a variety of sensory-based activities to conduct with children.

Daly, Lisa, and Miriam Beloglovsky. 2014. *Loose Parts: Inspiring Play in Young Children*. St. Paul, MN: Redleaf.

> This book provides many ideas for human-made loose parts to integrate into your preschool classroom.

Danks, Fiona, and Jo Scofield. 2007. *Nature's Playground: Activities, Crafts, and Games to Encourage Children to Get Outdoors*. Chicago, IL: Chicago Review Press.

> The book provides games, crafts, and other activities based on the seasons. Most of the ideas involve using natural loose parts.

Johnson, Kelly. 2017. *Wings, Worms, and Wonder: A Guide for Creatively Integrating Gardening and Outdoor Learning into Children's Lives.* 2nd edition. North Charleston, SC: CreateSpace.

This book delves into the world of gardening and provides tips and suggestions for gardening successfully with children.

Lingelbach, Jennipher, and Lisa Purcell. 2000. *Hands-On Nature: Information and Activities for Exploring the Environment with Children.* Woodstock, VT: Vermont Institute of Natural Science.

Using five themes (designs of nature, cycles, earth and sky, habitats, and adaptations), this book provides activity ideas for learning about nature.

Nelson, Eric. 2012. *Cultivating Outdoor Classrooms: Designing and Implementing Child-Centered Learning Environments.* St. Paul, MN: Redleaf.

This book provides ideas for moving indoor activities to your outdoor classroom.

Parrella, Deborah. 1995. *Project Seasons: Hands-On Activities for Discovering the Wonders of the World.* Shelburne, VT: Shelburne Farms.

This book provides seasonally based activities for kindergarten through sixth grade, but the information and ideas can easily be adapted to a younger audience.

Schlitz Audubon Nature Center. n.d. *Naturally Developing Young Brains.* Milwaukee, WI: Brain Insights. www.braininsightsonline.com

These flashcards on a ring each provide an activity idea on one side and insight into the benefits of that activity on the other side.

Selly, Patty Born. 2017. *Teaching STEM Outdoors: Activities for Young Children.* St. Paul, MN: Redleaf.

After describing STEM in the early years and children's need for nature, this book provides tools for thoughtfully reflecting on and implementing STEM learning outdoors.

Staff of Dodge Nature Preschool. n.d. *Four Seasons at a Nature-Based Preschool.* West St. Paul, MN: Dodge Nature Preschool. http://www.dodgenaturecenter.org/Preschool/Educator-and-Online-Resources/

This book, written by the teaching staff of Dodge Nature Preschool in West St. Paul, Minnesota, provides seasonally based activity suggestions. While the book is based on the natural features of the upper Midwestern region of United States, many of the activities are applicable for any geography.

Claire Warden's Fascination series:

- Warden, Claire. 2011. *Fascination of Air: Wind.* Auchterarder, UK: Mindstretchers.
- Warden, Claire. 2011. *Fascination of Earth: Wood Whittling.* Auchterarder, UK: Mindstretchers.
- Warden, Claire. 2011. *Fascination of Fire: Charcoal.* Auchterarder, UK: Mindstretchers.

- Warden, Claire. 2011. *Fascination of Water: Puddles.* Auchterarder, UK: Mindstretchers.

  This series of books provides vivid images and information to raise the skill level of nature-based teachers in engaging children with each activity discussed.

Wilson, Ruth. 2016. *Learning Is in Bloom: Cultivating Outdoor Explorations*. Lewisville, NC: Gryphon House.

  Ruth Wilson, a leader in the early childhood environmental education movement, provides a variety of activity ideas for indoors and outdoors, both on and away from school grounds.

Appendix B:
RESOURCES FOR DEVELOPING YOUR NATURAL PLAY AREA

Information

Bienenstock Natural Playgrounds
www.naturalplaygrounds.ca/resources-and-support

> This is the website of natural play-area designer Adam Bienenstock. It includes resources and support for developing natural play areas.

Danks, Sharon. 2010. *Asphalt to Ecosystems: Design Ideas for Schoolyard Transformation.* Oakland, CA: New Village Press.

> Full of beautiful imagery of schoolyard transformations and case studies from around the world, this book is sure to inspire.

DeBord, Karen, et al. 2005. *POEMS: Preschool Outdoor Environment Measurement Scale.* Lewisville, NC: Kaplan Early Learning Company. www.kaplanco.com

> Designed as a self-study, this scale is intended to raise the quality of outdoor children's environments and promote their use in teaching, research, and practice.

Keeler, Rusty. 2008. *Natural Playscapes: Creating Outdoor Play Environments for the Soul.* Lincoln, NE: Exchange Press.

> Written by one of the early leaders in natural play areas, this book provides a plethora of images and ideas for creating engaging play spaces for children.

Keeler, Rusty. 2016. *Seasons of Play: Natural Environments of Wonder.* Lewisville, NC: Gryphon House.

> This book illustrates how to design natural play environments that encourage exploration and creativity in all seasons of the year.

Moore, Robin. 1993. *Plants for Play: A Plant Selection Guide for Children's Outdoor Environments.* Berkeley, CA: Mig Communications.

> This book does exactly what you would expect: it provides ideas for appropriate plant selection for natural play areas.

Moore, Robin. 2014. *Nature Play and Learning Places: Creating and Managing Places Where Children Engage with Nature.* Raleigh, NC: North Carolina State University College of Design Natural Learning Initiative. http://natureplayandlearningplaces.org/wp-content/uploads/2014/09/Nature-Play-Learning-Places_v1.2_Sept22.pdf

> This book provides guidelines for engaging children of all ages with nature in a variety of settings—both in and out of school.

Moore, Robin, Susan Goltsman, and Daniel Iacofano. 1992. *The Play for All Guidelines: Planning, Design, and Management of Outdoor Play Settings for All Children*. Berkeley, CA: Mig Communications.

These guidelines were written for designers and community planners. It may be a useful resource if you are working with a landscape architect or builder to develop a natural play area.

Natural Learning Initiative. College of Design, North Carolina State University. https://naturalearning.org

This website offers design ideas, research, and resources.

Inspiration and Supplies

Community Playthings
www.communityplaythings.com

The Outlast line is made to withstand the elements outdoors—and it does.

Nature Explore
https://natureexplore.org

A website with natural play-area resources for purchase or inspiration.

Nature's Instruments
www.naturesinstruments.com

A retailer of natural play-area elements, including items for music play, sand and water play, and more.

Natural Playgrounds Company
www.naturalplaygrounds.com

A variety of music, art, science, and sensory-based elements for natural play areas.

NATURE-BASED EDUCATIONAL SUPPLIES

Acorn Naturalists
www.acornnaturalists.com

> They offer just about anything nature-related you can think of.

BioQuip
www.bioquip.com

> This is a great resource for pond dippers.

Carolina Biological Supply Company
www.carolina.com

> This site has a variety of tools for exploring environmental and life sciences.

Crazy Crow Trading Post
www.crazycrow.com

> This is a great resource for animal furs.

Explorations Early Learning
www.explorationsearlylearning.com

> A good place to find wood blocks, beads, and lacing slabs.

Forestry Suppliers
www.forestry-suppliers.com

> This site offers a variety of equipment and tools for exploring nature. Check out the "science education" section.

Nature Explore
www.natureexplore.org

> Their outdoor fabric is great.

Nature Watch
www.nature-watch.com

> Offers a variety of nature-based educational products, including craft kits.

Rhode Island Novelty
www.rinovelty.com

> A good source for fabric dress-up animal wings. (Tip: Search for "plush wings.")

Skulls Unlimited
www.skullsunlimited.com

> Just as the name implies, they sell animal bones, claws, and teeth.

Inexpensive or Free Supplies

Don't forget, there are many free or inexpensive supplies available for use in nature exploration. Here are a few ideas to get you started:

- 2-liter pop bottles
- 5-gallon buckets
- basters
- bedsheets
- bowls
- colanders
- paint-color sample cards
- crayons
- dirt
- egg cartons
- flashlights
- garden hoses
- gardening trowels
- ice cream scoops
- leaves
- mirrors
- paper
- plastic jars
- pencils
- pie tins
- pillowcases
- plastic tarps
- rocks
- ropes
- sheets
- shovels
- sponges
- spoons
- sticks

REFERENCES AND RECOMMENDED READING

AAP Council on Communications and Media. 2016. "Media and Young Minds." *Pediatrics* 138(5): e20162591.

Antioch University–New England. 2018. "Certificate in Nature-Based Early Childhood Education." Antioch University–New England. https://www.antioch.edu/new-england/degrees-programs/education/nature-based-early-childhood-education-certificate/

Bailie, Patti. 2010. "From the One-Hour Field Trip to a Nature Preschool: Partnering with Environmental Organizations." *Young Children* 65(4): 76–82.

Bailie, Patti. 2012. "Connecting Children to Nature: A Multiple Case Study of Nature Center Preschools." Doctoral diss. Lincoln, NE: University of Nebraska–Lincoln. https://digitalcommons.unl.edu/cgi/viewcontent.cgi?article=1028&context=teachlearnstudent

Ball, David, Tim Gill, and Bernard Spiegal. 2014. "Risk-Benefit Assessment Form." Bristol, UK: Play England, Play Scotland, Play Wales, and PlayBoard Northern Ireland. http://www.playengland.org.uk/resource/risk-benefit-assessment-form/

Ball, David, Tim Gill, and Bernard Spiegal. 2008. *Managing Risk in Play Provision: Implementation Guide.* Bristol, UK: Play England. http://eprints.mdx.ac.uk/5027/1/managing-risk-play-provision-guide.pdf

Chawla, Louise. 1988. "Children's Concern for the Natural Environment." *Children's Environments Quarterly* 5(3): 13–20.

Chawla, Louise. 1999. "Life Paths into Effective Environmental Action." *Journal of Environmental Education* 31(1): 15–26.

Children and Nature Network. 2018. "Children and Nature Network" (homepage). Children and Nature Network. https://www.childrenandnature.org/

Copple, Carol, and Sue Bredekamp, eds. 2009. *Developmentally Appropriate Practice in Early Childhood Programs Serving Children from Birth through Age 8.* 3rd ed. Washington, DC: National Association for the Education of Young Children.

Davis, Julie, and Sue Elliott, eds. 2014. *Research in Early Childhood Education for Sustainability: International Perspectives and Provocations.* Abingdon, UK: Routledge.

Dewey, John. 1938. *Experience and Education.* New York, NY: Simon and Schuster.

Duncan, Sandra, Jody Martin, and Rebecca Kreth. 2016. *Rethinking the Classroom Landscape: Creating Environments That Connect Young Children, Families, and Communities.* Lewisville, NC: Gryphon House.

Edwards, Carolyn, Lella Gandini, and George Forman, eds. 2012. *The Hundred Languages of Children: The Reggio Emilia Experience in Transformation.* 3rd ed. Santa Barbara, CA: Praeger.

Faber Taylor, Andrea, and Frances Kuo. 2009. "Children with Attention Deficits Concentrate Better after Walk in the Park." *Journal of Attention Disorders* 12(5): 402–409.

Faber Taylor, Andrea, Frances Kuo, and William Sullivan. 2001. "Coping with ADD: The Surprising Connection to Green Play Settings." *Environment and Behavior* 33(1): 54–77.

Finch, Ken, and Patti Bailie. 2015. "Nature Preschools: Putting Nature at the Heart of Early Childhood Education." *Occasional Paper Series* 2015(33): 95–104. https://educate.bankstreet.edu/occasional-paper-series/vol2015/iss33/9

Fjørtoft, Ingunn. 2001. "The Natural Environment as a Playground for Children: The Impact of Outdoor Play Activities in Pre-Primary School Children." *Early Childhood Education Journal* 29(2): 111–117.

Fritz, Regina Wolf, Kirsten Smyrni, and Katie Roberts. 2014. "The Challenges of Bringing the Waldkindergarten Concept to North America." *Children, Youth, and Environments* 24(2): 215–227.

Froebel, Friedrich. 1887. *The Education of Man.* New York, NY: D. Appleton.

Gill, Tim. 2007. *No Fear: Growing Up in a Risk-Averse Society.* London, UK: Calouste Gulbenkian Foundation. https://timrgill.files.wordpress.com/2010/10/no-fear-19-12-07.pdf

Gill, Tim. 2014. "The Benefits of Children's Engagement with Nature: A Systematic Literature Review." *Children, Youth, and Environments* 24(2): 10–34.

Gorman, Michele. 2015. "Yogi Berra's Most Memorable Sayings." Newsweek. https://www.newsweek.com/most-memorable-yogi-isms-375661

Graue, M. Elizabeth, Kristin Whyte, and Anne Karabon. 2015. "The Power of Improvisational Teaching." *Teaching and Teacher Education* 48: 13–21.

Green Hearts Institute for Nature in Childhood. 2014. "Nature Preschools: What Is a Nature Preschool?" Green Hearts Institute for Nature in Childhood. http://www.greenheartsinc.org/Nature_Preschools.html

Hanscom, Angela. 2016. *Balanced and Barefoot: How Unrestricted Outdoor Play Makes for Strong, Confident, and Capable Children.* Oakland, CA: New Harbinger Publications.

International Association of Nature Pedagogy. n.d. "Nature Pedagogy International Association" (homepage). International Association of Nature Pedagogy. https://www.naturepedagogy.com

Kahn, Peter, Thea Weiss, and Kit Harrington. 2018. "Modeling Child-Nature Interaction in a Nature Preschool: A Proof of Concept." *Frontiers in Psychology* 9(835): 1–16.

Katz, Lilian. 2010. "STEM in the Early Years." Paper presented at the SEED (STEM in Early Education and Development) Conference, Cedar Falls, IA. http://ecrp.uiuc.edu/beyond/seed/katz.html

Keeler, Rusty. 2016. *Seasons of Play: Natural Environments of Wonder.* Lewisville, NC: Gryphon House.

Kenny, Erin. 2013. *Forest Kindergartens: The Cedarsong Way.* Vashon, WA: Cedarsong Nature School.

Klemmer, Cynthia, Tina Waliczek, and Jayne Zajicek. 2005. "Growing Minds: The Effect of a School Gardening Program on the Science Achievement of Elementary Students." *HortTechnology* 15(3): 448–452.

Milteer, Regina, et al. 2012. "The Importance of Play in Promoting Healthy Child Development and Maintaining Strong Parent-Child Bond: Focus on Children in Poverty." *Pediatrics* 129(1): e204–e213.

Larimore, Rachel. 2011a. *Establishing a Nature-Based Preschool*. Fort Collins, CO: National Association for Interpretation.

Larimore, Rachel. 2011b. "Nature-Based Preschools: A Powerful Partnership between Early Childhood and Environmental Education." *Legacy Magazine* 22(3): 8–11.

Larimore, Rachel. 2016. "Defining Nature-Based Preschools." *International Journal of Early Childhood Environmental Education* 4(1): 32–36.

Larimore, Rachel, et al. August 2–5, 2017. "Children's Development in a Nature-Based Preschool Compared to a Traditional Preschool Setting." Poster presented at the Nature-Based Preschool National Conference, Seattle, WA. http://www.rachel-larimore.com/blog/2017/9/1/research-poster-presented-at-nature-based-preschool-national-conference-2017

Marcon, Rebecca. 2002. "Moving up the Grades: Relationship between Preschool Model and Later School Success." *Early Childhood Research and Practice* 4(1): n.p. http://ecrp.uiuc.edu/v4n1/marcon.html

Montessori, Maria. 1912. *The Montessori Method*. 2nd ed. New York, NY: Frederick A. Stokes.

Mooney, Carol. 2000. *Theories of Childhood: An Introduction to Dewey, Montessori, Erikson, Piaget, and Vygotsky*. St. Paul, MN: Redleaf.

Moore, Robin. 2014. *Nature Play and Learning Places: Creating and Managing Places Where Children Engage with Nature*. Raleigh, NC: Natural Learning Initiative and National Wildlife Federation. http://www.abcee.org/cms/wp-content/uploads/2014/11/Nature-Play-Learning-Places_v1.1.pdf

Natural Start Alliance. [in press]. "Generating Policies and Procedures for Nature-Based Experiences at Your Site" [working title]. Natural Start Alliance. https://naturalstart.org

Nicholson, Simon. 1972. "The Theory of Loose Parts: An Important Principle for Design Methodology." *Studies in Design Education Craft and Technology* 4(2): 5–14.

North American Association for Environmental Education. 2017. *Nature Preschools and Forest Kindergartens: 2017 National Survey*. Washington, DC: North American Association for Environmental Education. http://naturalstart.org/sites/default/files/staff/nature_preschools_national_survey_2017.pdf

North American Association for Environmental Education. 2018. "Natural Start Alliance" (homepage). Natural Start Alliance. https://naturalstart.org/

North American Butterfly Association. 2017. "Butterfly Questions and Answers." North American Butterfly Association. www.naba.org/qanda.html

Northern Illinois Nature Preschool Association. n.d. "Northern Illinois Nature Preschool Association" (homepage). Northern Illinois Nature Preschool Association. https://ninpa.org/

Pelo, Ann. 2013. *The Goodness of Rain: Developing an Ecological Identity in Young Children*. Redmond, WA: Exchange.

Rideout, Victoria, Ulla Foehr, and Donald Roberts. 2010. *Generation M2: Media in the Lives of 8- to 18-Year-Olds*. Menlo Park, CA: Henry J. Kaiser Family Foundation. https://files.eric.ed.gov/fulltext/ED527859.pdf

Rivkin, Mary, and Deborah Schein. 2014. *The Great Outdoors: Advocating for Natural Spaces for Young Children*. Rev. ed. Washington, DC: National Association for the Education of Young Children.

Rose, Kathryn, et al. 2008. "Outdoor Activity Reduces the Prevalence of Myopia in Children." *Ophthalmology* 115(8): 1279–1285.

Sandseter, Ellen. 2009. "Affordances for Risky Play in Preschool: The Importance of Features in the Play Environment." *Early Childhood Education Journal* 36(5): 439–446.

Sandseter, Ellen. 2009. "Characteristics of Risky Play." *Journal of Adventure Education and Outdoor Learning* 9(1): 3–21.

Schein, Deborah. 2014. "Nature's Role in Children's Spiritual Development." *Children, Youth, and Environments* 24(2): 78–101.

Selly, Patty. 2014. *Connecting Animals and Children in Early Childhood*. St. Paul, MN: Redleaf.

Sobel, David. 2013. *Beyond Ecophobia: Reclaiming the Heart in Nature Education*. 2nd ed. Great Barrington, MA: Orion Society.

Sobel, David. 2014. "Learning to Walk between the Raindrops: The Value of Nature Preschools and Forest Kindergartens." *Children, Youth, and Environments* 24(2): 228–38.

Sobel, David, et al. 2016. *Nature Preschools and Forest Kindergartens: The Handbook for Outdoor Learning*. St. Paul, MN: Redleaf.

Stipek, Deborah, et al. 1995. "Effects of Different Instructional Approaches on Young Children's Achievement and Motivation." *Child Development* 66(1): 209–223.

Tandon, Pooja, Brian Saelens, and Dimitri Christakis. 2015. "Active Play Opportunities at Child Care." *Pediatrics* 135(6): e1425–e1431.

Vygotsky, Lev. 1978. *Mind in Society: The Development of Higher Psychological Processes*. Cambridge, MA: Harvard University Press.

Warden, Claire. Forthcoming. "Nature Pedagogy: The Art of Being with Nature Inside, Outside, and Beyond." Doctoral diss. Liverpool, UK: Liverpool Hope University.

Warden, Claire. 2012a. *Nature Kindergartens and Forest Schools: An Exploration of Naturalistic Learning within Nature Kindergartens and Forest Schools* 2nd ed. Auchterarder, UK: Mindstretchers.

Warden, Claire. 2012b. *Talking and Thinking Floorbooks: Using "Big Book Planners" to Consult Children*. 2nd ed. Auchterarder, UK: Mindstretchers.

Warden, Claire. 2015. *Learning with Nature: Embedding Outdoor Practice*. London, UK: SAGE.

Wells, Nancy, and Gary Evans. 2003. "Nearby Nature: A Buffer of Life Stress among Rural Children." *Environment and Behavior* 35(3): 311–330.

Wilson, Edward. 1984. *Biophilia*. Cambridge, MA: Harvard University Press.

Wu, Pei-Chang, et al. 2013. "Outdoor Activity during Class Recess Reduces Myopia Onset and Progression in School Children." *Ophthalmology* 120(5): 1080–1085.

INDEX